The American Juvenile Justice System

LAW AND CRIMINAL JUSTICE SERIES

Series Editor: James A. Inciardi
Division of Criminal Justice, University of Delaware

The **Law and Criminal Justice Series** provides students in criminal justice, criminology, law, sociology, and related fields with a set of short textbooks on major topics and subareas of the field. The texts range from books that introduce the basic elements of criminal justice for lower-division undergraduates to more advanced topics of current interest for advanced undergraduates and beginning graduate students. Each text is concise, didactic, and produced in an inexpensive paperback as well as hardcover format. Each author addresses the major issues and areas of current concern in that topic area, reporting on and synthesizing major research done on the subject. Case examples, chapter summaries, and discussion questions are generally included in each volume to aid in classroom use. The modular format of the series provides attractive alternatives to large, expensive classroom textbooks and timely supplements to more traditional class materials.

Other volumes in this series:

Additional volumes currently in development.

The American Juvenile Justice System

GENNARO F. VITO
DEBORAH G. WILSON

Preface by J. PRICE FOSTER

Volume 5.
Law and Criminal Justice Series

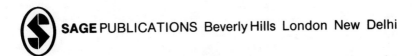 **SAGE** PUBLICATIONS Beverly Hills London New Delhi

For information address:

SAGE Publications, Inc.
275 South Beverly Drive
Beverly Hills, California 90212

SAGE Publications India Pvt. Ltd.
M-32 Market
Greater Kailash I
New Delhi 110 048 India

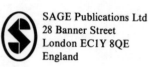

SAGE Publications Ltd
28 Banner Street
London EC1Y 8QE
England

Printed in the United States of America

Library of Congress Cataloging in Publication Data

Vito, Gennaro F.
  The American juvenile justice system.

  (Law and criminal justice series ; v. 5)
  Includes index.
  1. Juvenile justice, Administration of—United States.
2. Juvenile delinquency—United States. 3. Rehabilitation
of juvenile delinquents—United States. I. Wilson,
Deborah G. II. Title. III. Series.
HV9104. V58   1985   364.3'6'0973   85-14571
ISBN 0-8039-2318-X)
ISBN 0-8039-2319-8 (pbk.)

FIRST PRINTING

CONTENTS

PREFACE

Since the decade of the 1960s, when crime and civil disorder emerged as the first priority of national concern and public policy, there has been an increasing appreciation of highly trained professionals in the wide array of skills associated with the field.

This need was recognized early by Congress, and since the inception of the Law Enforcement Assistance Administration and its predecessor, the Office of Law Enforcement Programs, funds were made available for training persons working in the field. The emphasis during the first several years was, predictably, directed toward upgrading the policing function. However, in 1974 Congress recognized the particular need to commit funds to the juvenile justice and delinquency prevention effort and authorized the creation of the Office of Juvenile Justice and Delinquency Prevention (OJJDP).

Throughout the history of federal involvement with improvements in criminal and juvenile justice, as well as the prevention of crime and delinquency, our institutions of higher education have been given the important responsibility of taking the lead in research and developing the body of knowledge associated with improvement in the field. This was so important to Congress in creating OJJDP that a special research arm was authorized as a part of that office. The National Institute for Juvenile Justice and Delinquency Prevention has as its primary mandate training, research, and technical assistance for the juvenile aspect of crime-related concerns.

It is equally certain that this research must be reported in such a way that we maximize the opportunities for the research to influence policy and practice. This volume fulfills in a very significant and timely fashion this latter need.

I am most pleased to have scholars such as Drs. Vito and Wilson on the faculty of the School of Justice Administration at the University of Louisville. They have succeeded in a collaborative effort of the highest quality, and we will all certainly benefit from this as well as other research and writings in which they are involved.

Congratulations to James A. Inciardi for his success as series editor and to those who have contributed to the series. We are all grateful for your efforts.

—J. Price Foster
Dean, School of Justice Administration,
University of Louisville

ACKNOWLEDGMENTS

This book is the result of a collaborative effort by the authors, and, for this reason, our names appear alphabetically. We bear primary responsibility for the chapters as follows: Dr. Vito, Chapters 2, 5, and 6, and Dr. Wilson, Chapters 1, 3, and 4. Our intention was to prepare a basic textbook which would outline the stages in the juvenile justice process, while presenting current critical issues facing the juvenile justice system.

We would like to express our appreciation to our friends and colleagues who assisted us in the preparation of this text. Mrs. Candalyn Fryrear tirelessly typed and prepared several copies and versions of the manuscript. Brian Callan prepared figures and tables for the text. Professor John C. Klotter provided materials and guidance on the interpretation of legal decisions. Drs. Harry E. Allen and Edward J. Latessa offered materials and tips that aided our analysis and writing. Finally, we would like to express our gratitude to Dr. James A. Inciardi and to Sage Publications for providing us with the opportunity to publish this text.

—G.F.V.
D.G.W.

1

DEFINING THE SCOPE
OF JUVENILE JUSTICE

DEFINITION OF DELINQUENCY

"Juvenile delinquency" is one of a great number of terms that we all use freely, assuming that we know that the term means; but do we? What is juvenile delinquency? Who are the juvenile delinquents?

Phillip and Bill were bored one evening. They took their father's car, without his permission, and drove around the suburbs of Birmingham. Periodically they would veer off the street and run across the front lawn of a house—"lawn hopping" they called it. Are they delinquents? Edward was first arrested for burglary when he was fourteen. He and his older brother John, who was seventeen, had committed eleven acts of burglary. Are they juvenile delinquents? Amy and Mary, both sixteen years old, come from upper middle-class families. They receive generous allowances from their parents each week. However, they regularly go to the shopping mall on Saturday and shoplift, never anything of extreme value—inexpensive jewelry, makeup, maybe a belt or scarf. Are they juvenile delinquents?

If these scenarios were read to a hundred people and each was asked to state who was a juvenile delinquent, the answers would be very different. "Juvenile delinquency" as an everyday term has no precise, agreed-upon definition. We all use it, and we all have our own personal definition, but our personal definitions are not always the same. The first task in our study of juvenile justice, then, is to try to define this term.

Juvenile delinquency is part of a larger category of behaviors that are contrary to the norms or social expectations of society. These behaviors, which depart from established social standards, are together called *deviance*. While many behaviors have been defined as deviant—such as adult crime, premarital sex, poor table etiquette—only a few are labeled as juvenile delinquency. This label is applied to behaviors that are deviant in two, not unrelated, ways. First, the term "juvenile delinquent" is a label applied to young people who commit acts that violate social norms. This is a very broad, general use of the term. Sometimes the acts that violate social expectations are illegal acts, such as theft, burglary, drinking under age, and vandalism. At other times the label is applied to legal yet less acceptable behavior, such as rowdyism, boisterous behavior at football games, hanging out in video arcades or public parks, and cruising shopping malls to meet members of the opposite sex.

The second application of the term is more precise and formal, the use of the term "juvenile delinquent" as a legal label. Under the law, the label "delinquent" is applied on the basis of three criteria: (1) It is applied on the basis of an individual's *age*. Each state has enacted in its statutes some age that is the distinguishing criterion between adult and juvenile. This age varies. In some states it is children under eighteen, in others it is children under seventeen, and in some it is children under sixteen. (2) The second criterion that governs the application of the label "juvenile delinquent" is *conduct*. The label may be applied only to behaviors defined by law. These behaviors always include acts that would be crimes if committed by an adult and status offenses, that is, acts that are illegal only if performed by a juvenile. These may include some combination of the following acts: truancy, being beyond the control of a parent or guardian, drinking under age, sexual promiscuity, running away, and knowingly associating wih criminals or immoral persons. (3) The final legal criterion is *adjudication*. The juvenile must be found to be delinquent by the juvenile court or some affiliate of the court. The behavior of the juvenile must be established as having, in fact, occurred, and it must be found to be an adult crime or status offense.

In most jurisdictions, juvenile delinquency is defined as "an act committed by a minor (an individual who falls under a statutory age limit . . .) that violates the penal code of the government with authority over the area in which the act occurred" (Senna and Siegel, 1981). While most state statutes would agree with this general definition of delinquency, there is a great deal of variation among specific definitions and requirements. For example, the maximum age for delinquency varies from state to state. A little over two-thirds of the states set eighteen as the maximum jurisdictional age, 20 percent set this age at seventeen, and 10 percent set it at fifteen (Davis,

1974). The result is that if two seventeen-year-olds commit the same crime in two different states, one may be tried as an adult and the other as a juvenile. Similarly, states vary in the provisions that determine when a juvenile, not older than the maximum age for juvenile court jurisdiction, may be tried as an adult. Some states, including Colorado, Hawaii, and Minnesota, will consider trying a juvenile as an adult only if the crime is a felony. Other states, such as Montana and Connecticut, specify certain crimes, such as Class A felonies or homicide, as crimes for which a juvenile may be tried as an adult. The states also vary in age limitations for this procedure. Some, such as Alaska, Oklahoma, and Maine, have no age restriction, only an act provision. Others set the age at anywhere from ten to seventeen years, depending on the crime committed (Bureau of Justice Statistics, 1983). As in the first example, the result is that two juveniles of the same age who commit the same crime in different states may have quite different experiences. One may be tried in juvenile court and the other in adult court; one will be sentenced as a child, the other as an adult.

Despite this variation between jurisdictions, the existence and application of juvenile delinquency statutes and provisions reflect a set of cultural beliefs and values about children. Today we classify and treat juvenile delinquents apart from adults because we believe that (1) children are different from adults, physically, emotionally, mentally, and intellectually; (2) because children are different from adults, they should be expected to behave differently than adults; and (3) children should be treated differently from adults. These beliefs underlying the philosophy, process, and organization of juvenile justice are recent historical developments. They are the product of a series of changing notions about children and childhood.

CHANGING PERCEPTIONS OF CHILDREN AND CHILDHOOD

Lloyd de Mause begins his book *The History of Childhood* (1974: 1) with this statement:

The history of childhood is a nightmare from which we have only recently begun to awaken. The further back in history one goes, the lower the level of child care, and the more likely children are to be killed, abandoned, beaten, terrorized, and sexually abused.

While de Mause is applying current standards of child care and treatment to the treatment of children in past centuries, his statement is quite insightful. Childhood and our beliefs about children are sociocultural constructs. That is, they are generated by a group of people at a given period in history. They are not absolutes but change as people, societies, and the experiences and circumstances of members of societies change. These conceptions of what children are, how they should act, and how they should be treated have gone through a series of changes throughout history.

Historians who have studied the history of childhood and children contend that childhood in a form similar to our current conceptions—as a time of learning, innocence, love, and tenderness—did not exist until the Middle Ages (Ariès, 1962; de Mause, 1974; Gillis, 1974). Instead, children were believed to be "little adults" and were treated as such. Childhood did not exist.

Until the Middle Ages, there was little value placed upon children. Infanticide was a regular practice in many, if not most, societies. Imperfect children—improperly shaped, deformed, sick, or less valued children (females)—were regularly killed. In fact, no law regulated infanticide until the fourth century A.D., when laws were passed in Greece and Rome in an effort to regulate the process. In the Middle Ages, infanticide of legitimate children in Western societies was dramatically reduced, but the infanticide of illegitimate children continued until the nineteenth century (de Mause, 1974).

The practice of abandonment, institutionalized and informal, is another form of treatment of children that reflects very different attitudes from those we hold currently. De Mause has posited that a transition from infanticide to abandonment of children developed as individuals from the fourth to the thirteenth century began to realize that children had feelings, emotions, "a soul," and therefore could less easily kill them and turned to abandonment as a mechanism of resolving their anxieties about child rearing. Whatever the reason, several practices such as wet-nursing (sending an infant for a stay of between two and five years to be nursed outside the home), the sale of children, fosterage (sending a child to be reared in another family until the age of seventeen), or apprenticeship (sending the child to live with another family while he learned a craft or profession), and the use of children as security for debts are examples of institutional-ized abandonment which reflect attitudes quite different from those we hold today.

Generally, until the Middle Ages, there was no childhood because there was no child. That is, there was no awareness of the different nature of children, mentally, intellectually, and emotionally. Children were mere adults in small bodies and were treated as such. Children were not portrayed in art until the thirteenth century, and then they were depicted as little adults. They had no distinct dress apart from adults until the thirteenth century, nor distinct games, hobbies, or pastimes (Ariès, 1962).

Children acted like and with adults, even in sexual matters. The idea that sexual references to and in front of children and sexual contact with and in front of children was improper is a concept that began to develop only in the Middle Ages, as the belief that children are different from adults developed. The "liberties which people took with children, by the coarseness of the jokes they made, and by the indecency of gestures made in public which shocked nobody and which were regarded as perfectly natural" (Ariès, 1962: 100) would be repugnant to most people today. For centuries, children were used sexually by adults. In Greece and Rome, young boys were used sexually by older men (de Mause, 1974). The sexual fondling of children was widely accepted, as well as the public display of sex acts by children with other children, themselves, or adults. Phillippe Ariès (1962) cites several entries from a source on Louis XIII in which his acts of exposing himself to others or their "jokingly touching [his] parts" was a form of amusement for the court.

Similarly, methods of child-rearing, especially punishment and control of children, have shifted dramatically. De Mause reported that his examination of two hundred statements on child rearing prior to the eighteenth century revealed that nearly all approved of the severe beating of children. One thirteenth-century law read, "If one beats a child until it bleeds, then it will remember, but if one beats it to death, the law applies" (de Mause, 1974: 42).

Precisely how and why attitudes toward children changed is a matter of debate among historians in this area. Many credit the

Christian reformists of the seventeenth century, who believed in the innocence and weakness of children, with initiating a shift in social conceptions (Ariès, 1962). Others mention population imperatives, such as the excess of male as opposed to female children when the practice of infanticide is acceptable and institutionalized, as contributing factors (de Mause, 1974). Additionally, changing philosophies of human nature, human rights, and the increased economic value of children as laborers are cited as trends that helped to effect the change (Kessen, 1965). Finally, scholars have also suggested that changes in living conditions and economic structures reduced infant and child mortality, reduced parental detachment, and increased identification with and special treatment of children (Gillis, 1974). Whatever the specific combination of trends and events, the Middle Ages was the beginning of the beliefs that (1) children are different from adults, (2) children in various ways are more innocent, more helpless than adults, and (3) children therefore should be identified as separate from adults and should be treated differently. This was the beginning of our current beliefs that children are more innocent, purer, weaker, more helpless, and in need of more specialized treatment than adults. This was the beginning of the "rise of the child from his older place as ill-formed adult at the edges of the society to his present position as cultural hero" (Kessen, 1965: 5).

THE PHILOSOPHY OF JUVENILE JUSTICE

Our current conceptions of children as impressionable, naive, dependent beings who need nurturance, guidance, understanding, and protection until they are ready to enter the adult world are central to the underlying philosophy of the juvenile justice system. This philosophy is embodied in the concept of *parens patriae,* literally, "the state is the father." The concept of parens patriae views children as easily impressed and influenced by others, and as individuals who engage in criminal acts because they have been in some way negatively affected by others through inadequate care, custody, or treatment. Criminal behavior is interpreted as a sign or symptom of some problem in the child's family relationships or environment. This, then, invites the intervention of the state, as parent, to exercise

p. 51

control over the youth before more serious consequences result. In its interventive role, according to this philosophy, the state acts as a parent with the best interests of the child as the primary consideration. The objective of the parental role is to care for and treat the child, rather than to punish, to achieve change in the child's behavior.

The philosophy of parens patriae encompasses the sociocultural belief that children are more innocent and impressionable than adults. Therefore, it assumes that children are less responsible for their acts than adults. This belief, that some categories of individuals are less responsible for their acts than the average adult, has been a basic tenet of criminal law since the early development of English common law in the eleventh century. Under English common law, which was the basis of the American legal system, children under the age of seven could not be tried for criminal offenses, because it was believed that they did not have the ability to be criminally responsible. More specifically, they did not have the capacity to have intent *(mens rea)* and therefore did not with criminal intention or purpose commit criminal acts. Children between seven and fourteen years of age were also deemed incapable of criminal responsibility but could be tried as adults if the court could demonstrate they knew the difference between right and wrong. Once a child was more than fourteen years old, he or she was held responsible as an adult and was liable for the same criminal offenses as an adult.

Many individuals viewed early English criminal law as quite harsh and oppressive. In an attempt to minimize the severity of the law, a Council of Chancery was created. This council was established as a dispute settlement body and was given the "prerogative of grace." The prerogative was a mechanism through which the council could use its discretion and apply the law less strictly to individuals who might unduly suffer under a strict application of the legal code. One group of individuals to which the prerogative of grace applied was children. This council eventually developed into a court with extensive discretion, and the prerogative of grace came to be the principle of parens patriae. This court, the early predecessor of our juvenile court, exercised guardianship over children and acted on their behalf.

These principles were introduced into American society through the adoption of English common law as the basis of our legal system.

However, it was not until the late nineteenth century, following a humanitarian movement in corrections and criminal justice and a "child-saving" movement, that a distinctive juvenile justice system with a specialized juvenile court came into being.

DIVERSION

Diversion is the process of limiting the amount of involvement a juvenile has with the formal organization and procedures of the criminal and juvenile justice systems. Diversion is, and has been, a central objective of juvenile justice. Initially, the purpose of the development of the juvenile court was to divert juveniles from the adult criminal justice system. Ironically, in the 1960s, the diversion of juveniles from formal processing within the juvenile justice system became a prominent goal of juvenile justice.

The more recent impetus for diversion is not that different from those beliefs which led to the creation of the juvenile court. The belief is that official processing has negative consequences for juveniles. It tends to stigmatize or label the juveniles as "bad," resulting in serious consequences for the juveniles. The basic tenets of this orientation toward juvenile justice are:

(1) Many juvenile offenses are responded to excessively—most juvenile delinquency involves nonserious acts.
(2) When a child is officially processed, he or she is stigmatized.
(3) The stigma has a negative effect on the child's self-concept and on the way others treat him or her.
(4) The effect on self may be to alter the child's self-concept to one of a bad or criminal person. The child may then seek out similar peers and may act in ways that confirm his or her self-expectations.
(5) The stigma may also limit the child's opportunity for conformity, because the community will respond negatively to the child. Consequently, some support systems that might aid in altering the child's behavior may be removed.

This procedure of diversion is not limited to any one segment of the juvenile justice system or to agents and agencies of the system.

Nonreporting of crimes by citizens is the main mechanism through which juveniles are diverted from the justice processing. Police also divert many, if not most, juveniles with whom they have contact before they perform an arrest or take the juvenile into custody.

While all units have the capacity to divert, one unit, intake, is usually viewed as the formal diversionary unit. Intake is usually performed by juvenile probation officers. The function of this unit is to determine whether a juvenile will be sent before the juvenile court and, if not, into whose custody the juvenile should be released (parents, foster care, a halfway house) and any programs in which the juvenile should participate (such as drug and alcohol abuse, programs, school, or mental health programs). Even though this unit functions as the designated diversion mechanism, keep in mind that many, in fact most, juveniles are never processed to this point. Out of 500 potential arrests, police make 200 contacts which produce 100 arrests. Of these, only 40 youths reach the intake stage (Nejelski and LaPool, 1974). Hence, of 500 possible arrests, only 8 percent reach intake. Most diversion, then, is informal and occurs without the operation of the intake unit.

The further one proceeds in the system, the more formal the process of diversion. However, each unit within the system has the capability of making a decision to remove the child at that point from formal processing. In fact, the emphasis on diversion has created numerous public and private organizations and facilities to which a juvenile may be diverted. Some examples are family counseling programs, halfway houses, Outward Bound, drug and alcohol rehabilitation and treatment centers, and restitution and community service programs.

YOUTH SERVICE BUREAUS

As a result of the movement toward diversion suggested by the 1967 President's Commission on Law Enforcement and the Administration of Justice, the National Council on Crime and Delinquency promoted the development of Youth Service Bureaus. A Youth Service Bureau is a "noncoercive, independent public agency established to divert children and youth from the juvenile justice system by

(1) mobilizing community resources to solve youth problems, (2) strengthening existing youth resources and developing new ones, and (3) promoting positive programs to remedy delinquency-breeding conditions" (Norman, 1972: 3). The National Council on Crime and Delinquency found only twelve agencies operating under the goals of the Youth Service Bureau concept in 1967.

The concept, spurred by increasing acceptance of the objectives and principles of diversion and federal, state, and local funds, caught on quickly. By 1970, all but ten states had Youth Service Bureaus, and by 1971, 150 Youth Service Bureaus were in operation, funded by more than $21 million in federal, state, local, and private monies (Howlett, 1973).

The objective of a Youth Service Bureau is to minimize the stigma produced by legal processing by providing a noncoercive atmosphere to which the juvenile may be referred for problem identification and problem resolution. Proponents of the Youth Service Bureau argue that most juveniles are status offenders and therefore more in need of social services than court processing. That they will not help themselves and so need to have agency help—specifically, agency assistance that can draw on the available yet uncoordinated services in the community.

The Youth Service Bureau is a referral agency for the courts, police, school, parents, and other social service agencies. The objectives are (1) service brokerage, (2) resource development, and (3) systems modification.

Service Referral. Staff and volunteers assist the client and his or her family in identifying client needs and problems. Plans or programs to resolve these problems are developed utilizing existing community services and agencies. The client is then monitored in terms of his or her progress through the programs.

Resource Development. Volunteers and staff must continually monitor community resources that might be utilized to service the bureau's clients. Gaps in service are documented and may be filled with short-term Youth Service Bureau programs. However, long-range solutions are sought by encouraging other agencies to expand services, add new services, or develop new service agencies.

Systems Modification. A final task of the Youth Service Bureau is to note and document the attitudes and practices of public agencies and communities that encourage misbehavior among youth. These are then communicated to the responsible agencies, which, as allies, should be encouraged to assist in system modification (Norman, 1972).

A major component of any Youth Service Bureau is in-house program evaluation and research to determine the effectiveness and efficiency of its operations. This is to be ongoing research and is to be used as a means of determining program alteration and direction (Norman, 1972).

THE JUVENILE JUSTICE SYSTEM: STRUCTURE AND PROCESS

The juvenile justice system is composed of a series of units. Each unit has a distinct purpose, which is related to the purposes of every other unit, ultimately to accomplish the goals of detection, adjudication, and rehabilitation and control of juvenile delinquents. The units of the juvenile justice system—the police, the juvenile court, and juvenile corrections—parallel those of the adult criminal justice system.

The first point of contact with the juvenile justice system, the police, acts to discover, detect, investigate, and take into custody or refer juveniles. The second component of the system is the juvenile court. The court performs adjudication and disposition as well as initial screening and referral to a nonjudicial or judicial disposition. In some jurisdictions, usually the larger jurisdictions, the juvenile court is a separate unit that hears only juvenile cases. In other jurisdictions, it is a court that hears many types of cases, such as probate, small claims and juvenile cases. The juvenile court consists of both juvenile probation and juvenile court. The probation unit makes decisions about a child's prehearing detention, predisposition screening (which determines, whether a child will have a judicial or nonjudicial disposition), and postjudicial disposition screening, to make recommendations for the form of disposition once the case has been decided in juvenile court. The court handles formal and informal hearings and determines the child's corrections placement if a finding of "delinquent" is reached. The last unit is juvenile corrections. The function of this unit is to alter the behavior of the delinquent. Juvenile corrections encompasses many private and public organizations and facilities, ranging from community-based corrections to maximum security facilities, with goals that vary from community treatment to treatment and incapacitation.

As a system, each unit performs an operation that affects the functioning of every other unit. Police decisions and investigative skills determine the numbers of juveniles referred for consideration to juvenile court. The decisions of probation officers, as part of the court, determine the numbers of juveniles referred to judicial and nonjudicial dispositions. The decisions of juvenile judges and probation officers determine the numbers of juveniles placed in various correctional alternatives. Moreover, the effectiveness of correctional alternatives influences the numbers of juvenile delinquents through repeat offenders, which affects the number of juveniles to whom police must respond. While it is not always a highly coordinated or cooperative interdependency, the system operates as a set of extremely integrated units. Each of these units will be discussed in greater detail in the chapters that follow.

CRITICAL ISSUE:
THE PROBLEM WITH DIVERSION

Several rationales have been used to justify the creation and continued support of various diversion programs and practices. The theoretical rationale, described earlier, is that drawn from labeling theory. Juveniles who are diverted can avoid the stigma associated with formal processing and the resultant change in self-image, associations, and behavior associated with the negative societal reaction to the stigma. Diversion, then, "prevents" secondary deviance and criminal career progression. Second, diversion allows juveniles to receive help who might otherwise not receive treatment. It can place children in agencies and programs which provide treatment not available in juvenile corrections. Third, diversion, allows agents of juvenile justice to use their discretion and make referral or release decisions based on criteria that might otherwise be ignored by the court. Fourth, diversion can reduce the caseload of the juvenile court by diverting nonserious cases (as are most cases involving juveniles) and so allow the court to concentrate its resources on more serious juvenile crime. Fifth, diversion is a less expensive alternative to court processing.

While these rationales are legitimate and seemingly appropriate, a great deal of concern has been expressed by various scholars and practitioners over the large scale and almost unquestioning acceptance of diversion and the consequent explosion of diversion agencies and programs in the early 1970s. These individuals suggest that the rationales for and effects of diversionary programs may not be as positive as we once believed them to be. Most of the objections to diversion fall within the the following categories:

(1) *Absence of evidence to prove stigmatization increases delinquency or diversion eliminates stigma.* Little empirical evidence exists to suggest that the tenets of labeling theory are valid—that is, that stigma produces further delinquency. Therefore, the effect of labeling by the criminal court may be overstated (Nejelski, 1976). Likewise, the diversion of a juvenile may simply substitute one stigma for another. Rather than bearing a delinquent label, the child may bear the stigma associated with treatment by a mental health or drug abuse agency or the stigma of affiliation with social welfare agencies (Klein, 1976). There is also no reason to believe that avoidance of the delinquent stigma will eliminate or minimize the effect of other stigmas many juveniles bear, such as those induced by poverty, poor school achievement, or abusive treatment. If stigmas have a negative effect, these will also have a negative influence on the behavior of the juveniles (Nejelski, 1976).

(2) *Increased discretion may mean increased abuse of discretion.* While some jurisdictions set standards for diversion, many do not and when standards do exist it is not mandatory that they be followed. Diversion decisions, because of their discretionary nature, may lead to overemphasis on extralegal factors such as age, race, and social class, or, as Lundman (1976) stated, "diversion will magnify rather than alleviate existing abuses."

(3) *Diversion may increase rather than decrease the numbers of juveniles under control of the state.* There is evidence to suggest that diversion results in the referral from court to diversion agencies of

juveniles who otherwise might have been released without conditions. For example, Nejelski (1976) reports that in a survey of directors of Youth Service Bureaus, 68 percent thought the primary goal of their program was diversion yet believed that only 25 percent of their clients were in "immediate jeopardy" of the juvenile court. Similarly, Gibbons and Blake (1976) and Klein et al. (1976) report that most juveniles referred to agencies other than the court were not those who would have gone to court but those who would have been released by police officers or the court if diversion programs were not in existence.

(4) *Diversion may subvert due process.* Diversion from juvenile court is never completely voluntary. In some instances it may, on the surface, appear to be so, but some element of state coercion is always involved. This is because the diversion is always in lieu of court processing—a strong coercive agent. Because diversion naturally involves coercion of the state, concern over the due process rights of juveniles is present. The nature of diversion requires removal from the system prior to a determination of guilt or innocence. The programs and agencies to which juveniles are diverted restrict their liberties and attempt to change their behaviors, yet the juveniles have not been found guilty and have none of the protections a court adjudication can provide. Additionally, many diversion decisions and decisions within the agencies and programs to which juveniles are diverted are administrative decisions. These decisions are not very visible, nor are legal mechanisms available to review these decisions (Nejelski, 1976). Consequently, the harsh treatment by the courts which diversion seeks to avoid may result in equally harsh though different treatment through diversion.

(5) *Diversion diverts attention away from needed reforms in the juvenile justice system.* Diversion has provided us with a panacea in the form of an alternative to juvenile court processing. The proponents of diversion saw many problems in the formal juvenile justice system and so created an alternative that would promote a bypass or avoidance of the formal juvenile court. The problems identified by the reformers are still present, because diversion has pacified a concerned constituency. Therefore, the necessary changes in juvenile court have not occurred and are not likely to occur as long as attention is distracted from the real problem (Nejelski, 1976).

(6) *There is no real evidence that diversion reduces recidivism.* Evaluative research on diversion programs has not been done to any great extent. What research is present has not been done well. However, what general research exists shows no prominent or consistent evidence to suggest that diversion reduces recidivism. As Gibbons and Blake (1976) have stated, "studies were plagued with small sample numbers, ambiguity about process elements, and other shortcomings. On balance, these evaluation studies stand as testimony to the need for large-scaled, sophisticated evaluation of new programs. Clearly, there is insufficient evidence . . . for one to have much confidence in diversion arguments and contentions."

What, then, do we do about diversion? Surely, there is a need to divert juveniles who might be harmed by formal processing, but placing juveniles under state control without due process, especially when they otherwise might have been released, and using questionable selection criteria only create new problems. What seems to be required is, first, an assessment of the diversion procedures and the efficiency and effectiveness of these procedures. Second, diversion policies and procedures should be standardized, regulated, and made more visible and open to review. Third, some application of due process and clarification of juvenile rights in this area is necessary to ensure fairness. Fourth, every effort should be made to ensure that the "net" is not "widened" and so more children brought under state control. Finally, our attention should not be drawn away from needed formal system reform. Both the formal and the informal systems of disposition can and should exist as well as undergo much-needed reform.

2

DETECTION, IDENTIFICATION, AND PREVENTION:
The Police

Traditionally, the police in the United States have been given two basic roles, which are often emblazoned upon their vehicles: to serve and protect the public. Wilson (1968b) defined the basic police discretionary power to arrest in two ways: to enforce the law or to maintain order (for a complete treatment of the nature of policing, see also Skolnick, 1964; Bittner, 1970; Reiss, 1971; Rubenstein, 1973; Goldstein, 1977; Black, 1980; and Klockars, 1985). The fundamental problem concerning the exercise of police discretion can be viewed in these terms (see Packer, 1968): Should the police be permitted to use those methods that will increase the effectiveness of crime control (the apprehension of offenders), or should the police be limited in their procedures to those methods that are consistent with the rights of individuals in a democratic society (due process of law)? When juveniles enter the picture, this dilemma becomes even more complex, as the police are expected to perform a social work role and act in the best interests of the juvenile. In this chapter, we will consider the role of the police in the juvenile justice process and their great impact upon the entire juvenile justice system.

FUNCTION AND ROLE OF THE POLICE
IN THE JUVENILE JUSTICE SYSTEM

The police are the gatekeepers of the entire criminal justice system. Due to their arrest powers, the police initially determine who enters

AUTHORS' NOTE: We gratefully acknowledge permission granted by Charles C Thomas, Publisher, to reprint portions of *Police Work with Juveniles and the Administration of Juvenile Justice* by J. P. Kenney et al., 1982.

the criminal process. For this reason, the manner in which arrest powers are exercised by the police has a great impact upon the latter stages of both the adult and the juvenile justice systems (Kenney et al., 1982: 165-166):

> By the exercise of discretion in accepting and formally processing a reported offense, the police determine the volume of crime and delinquency. And by the exercise of discretion the police determine whether an offender will be arrested and put into criminal justice processes, arrested and released without official action, arrested and referred to a nonjudicial or noncorrectional agency for processing, or released outright without any formal action other than the temporary detaining of the offender either in the field or in the police station.

With juveniles, however, the police are expected to make a substantially different decision and to spend time offering counseling and guidance—to "stop the offense and begin the process of correction" (Kobetz and Bosarge, 1973: 107). Since the police are often the first to intervene in such cases, officers must decide when and how to act, whether to act on the behalf of society or in the best interests of the child, and whether it would be best to dispose of the case in an informal ("curbstone counseling" with release to parents) or formal (hold for court disposition) manner.

Beginning with the apprehension of the offender, the dispositional alternatives available to the police in juvenile cases are outlined in Figure 2.1 (Kobetz and Bosarge, 1973: 143):

(1) release, accompanied by a warning to the child;
(2) release, accompanied by an official report describing the encounter with the juvenile;
(3) station adjustment (preadjudicative disposition), which may consist of:
   (a) release to parent or guardian, accompanied by an official reprimand,
   (b) release accompanied by referral to a community youth services agency for rehabilitation when such an agency exists in the community, or,
   (c) if an "umbrella" youth agency does not exist in the community, release accompanied by referral to a public or private social welfare or health agency;

(4) referral to the juvenile court intake division, without detention;
(5) referral to the juvenile court intake division, with detention.

In this process, the potential referral to the juvenile officer plays a central role. As we shall see, juvenile police bureaus were developed in an attempt to harness the discretionary power of the police and to provide some measure of treatment on behalf of the juvenile. The basic idea was that the juvenile officer, divorced from the emotion of the street, could exercise more objective and dispassionate judgment and thus provide some measure of consistency and fairness in the processing of juvenile cases (Kenney et al., 1982: 149-150).

In sum, the police, through the initial contact with the juvenile, determine the extent of the juvenile's further involvement with the juvenile justice system. In addition to detecting delinquency, the police have the additional role of attempting to prevent it. With their juvenile clients, the police are given the task of acting in their best interests while protecting the community from delinquent acts. The key issue is: How do the police exercise their discretionary power over juveniles?

Studies of Police Discretionary Powers with Juveniles

Given the many alternatives available to the police, the manner in which their discretion is exercised is an issue to which criminologists have given serious attention. Is the decision to arrest based upon personal or racial prejudice? Does the seriousness of the act or the prior record (formal or informal) enter into this decision? Are juveniles who commit offenses in groups more likely to be arrested and processed? Does police professionalism make objectivity and fairness more likely? These are the types of research questions that have been posed by studies of police practices with juveniles.

One of the earliest studies of police encounters with juveniles was conducted by Piliavin and Briar (1964). Their analysis was based upon nine months of observation of all juvenile officers in a metropolitan police department that served a city of approximately 450,000. They reported that the officers felt reluctant to expose youths to the stigmatization of arrest and the entire criminal process. It was discovered that the police were most likely to base the decision to arrest upon the offender's character: his or her group affiliation,

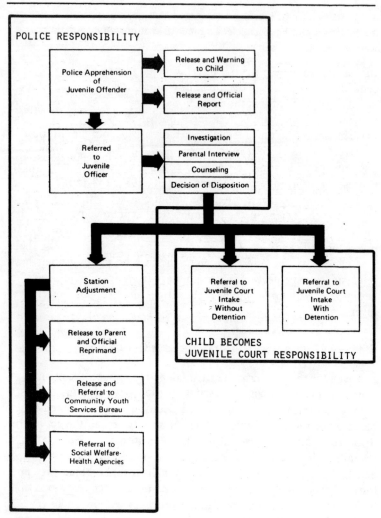

SOURCE: Kobertz and Bosarge, 1973. Reprinted by permission of the International Association of Chiefs of Police, Gaithersburg, Maryland.

Figure 2.1   Police-Juvenile Dispositional Alternatives

age, race, grooming, dress, and overall behavior. They tended to give more severe dispositions to blacks and to youths whose appearance was "tough." The officers felt the blacks were more likely to "give them a hard time," be uncooperative, and show no remorse for their transgressions. The officers also stated that they were well aware of this potentially prejudicial feeling but that it grew from their police experience. As the authors indicate, such a belief could have self-fulfilling consequences. Prejudices lead to closer surveillance of black districts, more frequent encounters with black juveniles, and more problems with this group. While Piliavin and Briar (1964: 213-214) noted that more due process mechanisms were necessary to guard against police misconduct at this level, they also noted that the "discretion practiced by juvenile officers is simply an extension of the juvenile court philosophy which holds that in making legal decisions regarding juveniles, more weight should be given to the juveniles' character and life situations than to his actual offending behavior." Of course, this is the basic problem with discretion at all levels of the criminal justice system. How can discretion be harnessed in such a way that fairness can be achieved without destroying the potential to make decisions on an individual, case-by-case basis?

For this reason, studies of police discretion and juvenile offenders have focused upon the issue of bias and prejudice. As we shall see, the results are mixed in terms of which particular factor plays the dominant role in the decision to arrest. Hohenstein (1969) examined the factors that resulted in delinquent events being brought to the attention of the Juvenile Aid Division of the Philadelphia Police Department. He discovered that the most important factor in the decision to sanction offenders was the attitude of the victim. If the victim did not seek prosecution, the offender was released. No evidence was found to support any claim of bias by the police in their disposition of juvenile offenders.

A similar study by Weiner and Willie (1971) focused upon the dispositional decision made by juvenile officers, rather than patrol officers, in two cities, Washington, D.C., and Syracuse, New York. Juvenile police officers were selected for study in this case because they determine whether the youth should be dismissed, sent to court, or referred to a social agency. The authors gave special attention to the race and socioeconomic status (SES) of the offenders. They reported that in Washington, the highest police contact and court referral rates were found in the lowest-ranked areas of SES, but that similar proportions of affluent and poor as well as black and white youths were referred to court. In Syracuse, they found that youths of high SES who lived in low SES tracts were most likely to be referred to court, possibly in an effort to "protect them from their environment" (Weiner and Willie, 1971: 206). There was no evidence of racial prejudice or bias in dispositions. Given the absence of police prejudice, the authors concluded that fairness may be an organizational norm of juvenile police bureaus that results from the manner in which individuals are selected for the job or one that develops in the bureaus themselves.

Another major study of police arrests of juveniles was conducted by Black and Reiss (1970). They also reported that they discovered no evidence of racial discrimination by the police. Although the arrest rates for black juveniles was higher than that of their white counterparts, this difference was due to factors other than race. The probability of arrest was strongly related to such variables as the seriousness of the offense, preferences of a complaining victim, the presence of situational evidence, and the "suspiciousness" of the juvenile (for example, acting unusually respectful or disrespectful). They also reported that the majority of police-juvenile encounters involved matters of minor legal significance.

This study was replicated by Lundman et al. (1980) with similar results. The authors reported that there was no evidence of racial discrimination in police arrest practices with juveniles. Again, they discovered that the great bulk of police work with juveniles involved diversion rather than arrest. The factors associated with arrest were (1) legal seriousness: all juveniles involved with a felony offense were arrested; (2) citizen preference: officers typically complied with the requests of citizens regarding the handling of juvenile offenders; (3) race: the high rate of arrest for black juveniles was attributable to black complainants who lobbied effectively for formal action by the police; and (4) demeanor: black and white juveniles who were antagonistic were arrested more frequently than juveniles who were civil, but those juveniles who were very deferential were also likely to be arrested, because their actions were regarded as suspicious (Lundman et al., 1980: 138-145). Given the almost identical findings of these two studies, it is clear that the police decision to arrest is affected by factors other than personal prejudice.

A survey of officer attitudes conducted by Hindelang (1976) also reinforces the pattern reported in these studies. He conducted a survey of 140 sheriff's deputies from a southwestern metropolitan area, posing a number of different situations involving juveniles and asking how they should be handled. Overall, he found that the majority of deputies preferred to deal with juveniles informally, but, once again, demeanor of the juvenile played a major role. If verbal abuse was present, even in cases of minor violations, the deputies favored arrest. The deputies also reinforced the widely held belief that juveniles who commit offenses in a group are more likely to be arrested and formally sanctioned.

As stated by Erickson (1973), the group hazard hypothesis states that the probability of arrest for juveniles increases when the offense is committed by a group rather than a single offender. This hypothesis has been tested in several other studies with some mixed results. Hindelang (1976) conducted a survey of 250 incarcerated juveniles to determine whether they committed delinquent acts alone or in a group. He reported that, although a substantial proportion of offenses (such as aggressive behavior) were committed always or usually alone, offenders who committed crimes as a group enterprise were more likely to be picked up by the police than those who committed delinquent acts in isolation. This pattern held true even when the seriousness and the frequency of the offenses in which the two groups had engaged were comparable. However, Feyerherm (1980) conducted a survey of 562 northeastern high school students and discovered that the group hazard hypothesis was more valid for theft crimes than for drug crimes and that the probability of apprehension by the police, rather than formal arrest, was enhanced by group activity. Yet Morash (1984) interviewed 588 delinquent youths from two Boston communities and found support for the group hazard hypothesis. She discovered that males with delinquent peers and those who engaged in group delinquent acts were most likely to have an arrest record, regardless of the frequency or seriousness of the offense. Overall, it appears that police arrest procedures are related to the group hazard hypothesis and that the visibility of the offense, plus the fact that other juveniles now have knowledge of it, increases the probability of arrest.

The last consideration is the effect of police professionalism upon juvenile arrest procedures. Wilson (1968a) compared the handling of juvenile offenders in two police departments. The first, in Eastern City, was characterized as a "fraternal" department in which officers were encouraged to make particularistic judgments about arrests, in which it was considered proper to take personal characteristics into account when dispensing justice, and in which training consisted mainly of "how to get along on the force." In contrast stands the Western City "professionalized" police department, which was organized along strict bureaucratic lines, with recruitment and promotion by achievement, training that considered the writings and teachings of experts, and the norm that laws should be enforced equally. With regard to juvenile arrest practices, however, Wilson (1968a:16) found that in the more professional Western City department, juveniles were more likely to come into contact with and to be arrested or cited by the police than in Eastern City, where reprimands or referrals were more common. Wilson believed that this finding was due to the fact that Eastern City police, who were likely to view delinquency as a problem of personal of familial morality and urged the use of punitive measures, were nonetheless more likely to release a juvenile unless a vicious crime had been committed. Due to the "bureaucratization" of the Western City department, officers were more likely to treat juveniles according to the rules and without regard to the person. Wilson's analysis questions the role of professionalism in police training and leads to the conclusion that norms of professionalization may make the police less discriminatory but more severe in their handling of juveniles.

In sum, these studies of police arrest practices with juveniles lead to several policy implications. The decision to arrest is affected by a number of factors. First, the character or demeanor of the juveniles is a key determining factor. If the juvenile is openly hostile or overly respectful, the juvenile is likely to be arrested. The police are also influenced by the attitude of the victim and will follow the preference of that individual regarding the handling of the case. Socioeconomic status also plays a major role in the arrest determination, as well as committing offenses in a group. Although most juvenile encounters with the police involve matters of "minor legal significance," the seriousness of the offense can also determine the decision by the police. There appears to be no hard evidence of racial discrimination; however, it could be that race is highly related to the key variables listed above.

Put simply, there appears to be no clear-cut answer to solving problems of arrest discrimination. These variables appear to be explained by the nature of the job faced by the police. A hostile juvenile who commits a group offense is likely to be arrested or at least approached. The police are not likely to bother with cases of minor seriousness unless a victim complains for action. Likewise, the police are unlikely to invest their time and energy if the victim is unlikely to take the steps necessary to sanction the juvenile. Professionalization of the police may lead to some unintended, negative side effects. Yet there is also evidence from the Weiner and Willie study that the use of specialized juvenile bureau officers may lead to a more balanced and nonprejudicial handling of juvenile cases. Of course, another key influence upon the decision to arrest is the rights of juveniles during police processes. A review of these rights demonstrates the due process safeguards which are designed to prevent abuses of police discretion.

RIGHTS OF JUVENILES
IN THE POLICE PROCESS

Basically, juveniles are afforded the same rights as adults in the criminal justice system by virtue of the *Gault* decision (1967). In fact, because of their vulnerability, juveniles may enjoy some additional protections. With regard to police processing, the rights of juveniles have received specific attention in the following stages (Wadlington et al., 1983: 267):

(a) the preliminary investigation ("stop and frisk" measures)
(b) the arrest process
(c) search and seizure
(d) questioning
(e) pretrial identification
(f) prehearing detention and release

The *Gault* decision expanded the rights of juveniles to ensure that their due process guarantees covered all aspects of the preadjudicatory process. It is largely held that certain procedural safeguards are especially necessary for juveniles because they are more vulnerable than adults.

Regarding the investigation process, the police may take juveniles into custody if probable cause is present. The requirement of probable cause exists for both arrests and warrants. Although many states permit juveniles to be taken into custody for their own protection and well-being, such arrests are intended to be a protective, rather than a punitive, form of detention, and they are not intended to avoid the traditional limits placed upon police arrest powers by the Constitution (Davis, 1974: 43). A common example, which had been subject to some changes, is status offenses (such as runaways). However, the courts have been quick to emphasize that the broad jurisdictional power enjoyed by the police in such cases should neither be abused nor be used as a method to circumvent constitutional rights where a child is taken into custody for what amounts to a criminal offense (Davis, 1974: 45). Typically, state statutes require that juveniles be treated in a special manner—for example, that parents, a probation officer, or the juvenile court be notified upon the apprehension of the juvenile (Paulsen and Whitebread, 1974: 79).

A key portion of the arrest process is the search of the person and the seizure of evidence pursuant to the arrest. Basically, the courts have ruled that the Fourth Amendment is applicable to juvenile arrest proceedings and that the exclusionary rule is applicable to unlawfully obtained evidence (Davis, 1974: 54-55). A "warrantless" search is justified only when (Paulsen and Whitebread, 1974: 80-81):

(a) the search is incident to a lawful arrest
(b) an on-the-street "stop and frisk" occurs
(c) the officer obtains the consent of the person searched
(d) it is necessary to prevent the destruction or removal of vital evidence

On-the-street stops of persons by the police can thus give rise to a restricted privilege to search without a warrant provided that a "reasonable suspicion" exists linking this person to a crime. Such searches are justified by the need for protection of the arresting officer and the public from any weapons involved in the crime.

In a special category of specific importance to juveniles, the searches and seizures conducted by public (or private) school officials have enjoyed a certain freedom from the restrictions placed upon the police. The courts have often ruled that the school official, as a private person, not an officer of the government and not subject to the Fourth Amendment, usually acts *in loco parentis* and has a special duty to maintain conditions of safety and discipline, which is far different from that of the police (Paulsen and Whitebread, 1974: 87-88; Wadlington, et al., 1983: 271-273). In 1985, the U.S. Supreme Court, in a 6 to 3 decision, ruled that school authorities need only a "reasonable suspicion" that their search will disclose evidence that a student broke the law or school rules. The Court held that such searches must be reasonably related to their objectives and not excessively intrusive in light of the age and sex of the student and the nature of the infraction (*New Jersey v. T.L.O.*, 1985).

However, recent Supreme Court decisions reveal that the police may also enjoy some changes in the provisions of the exclusionary rule. Rulings made by the Court in *United States v. Leon* (1984) and *Massachusetts v. Shepard* (1984) deal with cases in which search warrants were issued and police officers acted in "good faith" in the execution of the warrants. In both cases, the Court felt that the officers relied upon the determination of probable cause made by the magistrates involved and acted accordingly. This limited "good faith" exception could also apply to juvenile cases in the future.

In general, the interrogation of juveniles by police officers is subject to the same procedural guidelines established by the *Miranda* decision, which has its roots in the Fifth Amendment. Here, the crucial issue is: Can the juvenile make a knowing waiver of his or her rights without the aid of counsel or a parent? The general rule established by the courts (*West v. United States,* 1968) has been that a minor has the capacity to make a voluntary confession without the presence or consent of counsel or other responsible adult and that the admissibility of such a confession depends upon the "totality of circumstances" surrounding the admission, including (Davis, 1974: 93)

(a) age of the accused
(b) education of the accused
(c) knowledge of the accused of both the substance of the charge and the nature of his or her rights to consult with an attorney and remain silent
(d) whether the juvenile was held incommunicado or was allowed to consult with relatives
(e) whether interrogation was held before or after the filing of formal charges
(f) methods of interrogation

(g) length of interrogation
(h) whether the accused refused voluntarily to give statements on prior occasions
(i) whether the accused had repudiated an extrajudicial statement given at a later date

Thus, a juvenile is legally capable of waiving his or her rights under the Fourth, Fifth, or Sixth Amendment if these conditions are met and the child is able to comprehend the meaning and possible effect of any statements given to the police.

In addition, Paulsen and Whitebread (1974: 89-94) have outlined some basic requirements that have been established concerning the admissibility of statements and confessions made by juveniles. First, noting the "special vulnerability of children in the hands of the police," a statement made by a juvenile may not be used in juvenile court if it has been involuntarily given. Second, in some jurisdictions, confessions are inadmissible if the arresting officer fails to follow the statutory directives for making special disposition of a juvenile. Third, and most obvious, the custodial confession of a juvenile produced from an interrogation may not be used in juvenile court unless the required *Miranda* warnings have been given. The *Miranda* warnings should also be given to the parent of the juvenile, so that they may also protect the juvenile's Fifth Amendment rights. It may be that a child is able to waive the protection against self-incrimination only after a parent or guardian has offered some guidance on the subject.

A U.S. Supreme Court ruling in the case of *Fare v. Michael C.* (1979) gives us some indication of the ability of a juvenile to waive his or her rights. This case involved a murder in which the juvenile suspect, a person with a long juvenile history (he had been on probation since age twelve), made incriminating statements after asking to meet with his probation officer. Therefore, the central issue in the case was: Is a juvenile's request, made while undergoing custodial interrogation, to see his probation officer per se an invocation of the juvenile's Fifth Amendment rights under *Miranda*? The Court ruled that a probation officer is simply not necessary for the protection of the legal rights of the accused and that such an extension would impose the burdens associated with the rule of

Miranda on the juvenile justice system and the police without serving the interests that the rule was simultaneously designed to protect. In addition, the Court ruled that the request by the juvenile to speak with his probation officer did not constitute a request to remain silent, directing the police officers to stop the interrogation process. Therefore, the Court ruled that the statements made by the accused were admissible in court (Wadlington et al., 1983: 326-330).

Another Supreme Court case, involving an adult (*New York v. Quarles*, 1984), may have some far-reaching effect upon the rights of juveniles under the *Miranda* decision. In this case, police pursued a rape suspect, believed to be armed, into a supermarket. Upon apprenhension and before informing the suspect of his rights, the police officer asked the suspect where the gun was. The suspect pointed to some empty cartons and stated that "the gun is over there." The trial court excluded this and other statements at trial because the suspect had not yet been informed of his rights under *Miranda*. This decision was upheld by the Supreme Court of New York and the New York Court of Appeals. However, the U.S. Supreme Court ruled that there is a limited "public safety exception" to *Miranda*. In this case, "so long as the gun was concealed somewhere in the supermarket with its actual whereabouts unknown, it obviously posed more than one danger to the public safety: an accomplice might make use of it, a customer or employee might later come upon it." Therefore, the officers in this case were acting in the best interests of the public and did not seek to violate the rights of the suspect. The Court also indicated that this exception to requirements of *Miranda* is limited and that authorities must interpret it carefully.

Finally, with regard to pretrial identification and prehearing detention and release, juveniles possess some specific protections. In lineups, juveniles (via the *Gault* decision) have the same right to counsel as adults (Paulsen and Whitebread, 1974: 96-97; Davis, 1974: 96-100). In many states, the fingerprinting and photographing of juveniles during the booking process is subject to stringent restrictions because juveniles are viewed with care and ought to be protected from a criminal record (Davis, 1974: 99). Juveniles have the same rights as adults concerning bail, and "the statutory duty to notify the child's parents that he (or she) has been taken into custody is fairly typical" (Davis, 1974: 71-73).

In sum, it is clear that juveniles possess the same rights as adults in the police process and that they even enjoy some additional protections. Again, we see that the police are expected to treat and handle juveniles in a special manner, giving specific attention to their problems in an attempt to protect them from harm—either from their environment or from the juvenile justice system itself. In light of these legal and social requirements, police departments have developed specialized juvenile diversion units to remove juveniles from the system when it is possible to do so. These units and their operation form the critical issue for this chapter.

CRITICAL ISSUE:
THE SPECIALIZED JUVENILE
(DIVERSION) POLICE UNIT

It has long been recommended that, in light of the problems which juveniles face, "every police department should have a specialized juvenile unit, or in smaller departments, there should be at least one officer assigned specifically to the police-juvenile function" (Kobetz and Bosarge, 1973: 153). The advantages enjoyed or afforded by such a unit include (1) streamlining procedures for the juvenile court, receiving, and detention facilities; (2) development and use of community resources for the rehabilitation and treatment of delinquent youth; and (3) the building of knowledge of the problems of children (Kobetz and Bosarge, 1973: 154; Kenney et al., 1982: 206).

The juvenile police unit can dispose of cases brought to it in a number of ways, including (Kenney et al., 1982: 208-209):

(1) *Application for petition:* A petition means that the youth is subject to its jurisdiction and may be brought before the juvenile court.
(2) *Transfer of case:* Juvenile cases are transferred when another agency, such as a probation department, state training school, or other law enforcement agency, has jurisdiction.
(3) *Referral to other agencies:* A referral is made when it is believed that the case in question should be investigated further and some rehabilitative program set in motion for the guidance and adjustment of the juvenile to such agencies as the School Guidance and Welfare Bureau, Department of Social Welfare, family and children's agencies, or a diversion program.

(4) *Action suspended:* Action is suspended in cases where the parents and the juvenile, alone and unaided, can effect a satisfactory adjustment.

(5) *Finding insufficient evidence,* which results in the release of the juvenile.

(6) *Exoneration.*

(7) *Voluntary police supervision:* This disposition consists of furnishing guidance and counsel to the juvenile with the consent and full cooperation of the parents.

(8) *Finding that the "juvenile" proves to be an adult.*

(9) *Declaring the juvenile unfit:* This recommendation would apply when investigation discloses that the juvenile had committed an offense or offenses of a serious nature and that his or her previous record and attitude are such that a program of social treatment under the juvenile court would be ineffective.

(10) *Detention.*

The data in Table 2.1 reveal the manner in which police departments typically disposed of juvenile cases in 1983. Overall, the majority of cases (57.5 percent) were referred to the juvenile court jurisdiction—a pattern that was most predominant in the larger cities and the suburban and rural counties. A sizable percentage (32. 8 percent) were handled within the department and released—a disposition particularly favored in the mid-sized cities (population between 25,000 and 49,999) and the suburban areas. A small number of cases (4.8 percent) were referred to criminal or adult court.

However, the particular issue here is: How is the police decision to divert juveniles made? Shepard and Rothenberger (1980: 12) have defined police diversion is the following manner:

The Where. Diversion can take place at any point between a formally recorded apprehension and the formal acceptance of a petition by the juvenile court but not beyond the point of juvenile court intake.

The What. Diversion occurs when, in lieu of further juvenile justice processing, one of the following occurs:

(1) The youth is released to the custody of his or her parents or guardians.

(2) The youth volunteers to participate in a program designed to meet his or her needs.

TABLE 2.1

Police Disposition of Juvenile Offenders Taken into Custody, 1983

Population Group	Total	Handled Within Department and Released	Referred to Juvenile Court Jurisdiction	Referred to Welfare Agency	Referred to Other Police Agency	Referred to Criminal or Adult Court
TOTAL ALL AGENCIES: 8,360 agencies; population 162,976,000:						
Number	1,150,257	377,775	661,761	35,347	19,809	55,565
Percent	100.0	32.8	57.5	3.1	1.7	4.8
TOTAL CITIES: 5,690 cities; population 112,807,000:						
Number	979,967	325,560	555,934	32,869	17,552	48,052
Percent	100.0	33.2	56.7	3.4	1.8	4.9
Group I						
47 cities, 250,000 and over; population 30,436,000:						
Number	272,974	74,525	165,774	20,230	9,626	2,819
Percent	100.0	27.3	60.7	7.4	3.5	1.0
Group II						
107 cities 100,000 to 249,999; population 15,565,000:						
Number	123,074	41,290	76,771	2,502	757	1,754
Percent	100.0	35.5	62.4	2.0	.6	1.4
Group III						
228 cities, 50,000 to 99,000; population 15,565,000:						
Number	126,252	44,008	69,942	3,359	1,899	7,044
Percent	100.0	34.9	55.4	2.7	1.5	5.6

		Total					
Group IV							
510 cities, 25,000 to 49,999; population 17,682,000:							
	Number	161,534	61,233	85,783	3,504	1,940	9,074
	Percent	100.0	37.9	53.1	2.2	1.2	5.6
Group V							
1,224 cities under 10,000; population 19,230,000:							
	Number	173,406	63,589	92,757	2,007	1,851	13,202
	Percent	100.0	36.7	53.5	1.2	1.1	7.6
Group VI							
3,574 cities under 10,000; population 14,350,000:							
	Number	122,725	40,915	64,907	1,267	1,479	14,139
	Percent	100.0	33.3	52.9	1.0	1.2	11.5
Suburban Counties							
873 agencies, population 31,243,000:							
	Number	126,936	42,886	76,963	1,762	1,048	4,277
	Percent	100.0	33.8	60.6	1.4	.8	3.4
Rural Counties							
1,797 agencies; population 18,926,000:							
	Number	43,354	9,329	28,864	716	1,209	3,236
	Percent	100.0	21.5	66.6	1.7	2.8	7.5
Suburban Area							
4,082 agencies; population 74,492,000:							
	Number	495,064	197,044	252,279	7,916	5,295	32,530
	Percent	100.0	39.8	51.0	1.6	1.1	6.6

SOURCE: Uniform Crime Reports for the United States, 1983.
1. Includes all offenses except traffic and neglect cases.
2. Because of rounding, the percentages may not add to total.
3. Includes suburban city and county law enforcement agencies within metropolitan areas. Excludes core cities. Suburban cities and counties are included in other groups.

These authors caution that police diversion should be applied only in cases where there is a substantial likelihood that a conviction can be obtained and that diversion should not become a "dumping ground" for weak cases (Shepard and Rothenberger, 1980: 16). A survey by Vanagunas (1979) of a representative sample of 37 police agencies employing more than 200 officers revealed that only 24 percent of the departments stated that they had the responsibility for diversion. Among these agencies, the decision to divert seemed to be made upon "legalistic" (seriousness of the crime, prior record, quality of the evidence, and so on) rather than "rehabilitative" (needs of the youth) grounds. Based upon this evidence, Vanagunas (1979: 52) concluded that police administrators were not treating diversion of juveniles as a priority issue.

Naturally, the police diversion process can be plagued by the same problems to which diversion at any level can fall victim. In particular, the "widening of the net" problem, bringing in cases in order to divert them, is vexing. Therefore, the need for guidelines is particularly apparent. A number of criteria have been offered to guide the police diversion process, including (Shepard and Rothenberger, 1980: 29):

(1) nature of the offense
(2) age of the offender
(3) nature of the problem that led to the offense
(4) a history of contacts or use of physical violence
(5) character of the offender and history of behavior in school, family, and peer group settings

Typically, police diversion programs make two basic decisions: diversion without referral (directly to parents or guardian without the involvement of any other agency) or diversion with referral (to provide some type of treatment instead of referral to the court). These decisions parallel the structure of the police diversion unit. In-house programs operate totally within police departments with sworn officers, while outside referral programs require the coordination of local community resources to meet the needs of youth and often require the purchase of services.

A number of studies of the police diversion process have been conducted that give specific attention to the manner in which referrals were made and the type of case that was most likely to be diverted. For example, Klein (1976) examined the "explosion" of police diversion programs in an attempt to explain the phenomenon. Through interviews with juvenile officers in thirty-five police departments, Klein (1976: 108-109) discovered that the composite of the "more referable offender" was the

> young, minor offender with little or no record, who is unlikely to be arrested in any case. This picture fits the profile of the youngster who heretofore would have been released outright, for whom referral represents *increased* intervention, rather than diversion *from* system intervention. This evidence leads to the conclusion that police diversion is "widening the net" and that it represents a form of "alternative encapsulation"—exposing juveniles to another form of the juvenile justice system which is as threatening as the formal system itself.

However, the "widening of the net" in police diversion may be related to factors other than personal conveniences. A study by Sundeen (1976) examined the relationship between the professional and community attitudes of a police department and its rate of diversion referrals and discovered that these attributes alone did not explain the police diversion of juvenile training given to officers, the establishment of local friendships, and the amount of official resources available to the department.

The structure of the unit (in-house versus outside referral programs) was another variable considered in the attempt to explain the use of diversion by the police. Klein and Teilmann (1980) were primarily concerned with whether there was a difference between these types of programs with regard to the type of client diverted. They reported that, "so far as the departments were concerned, most are doing diversion because someone else wants them to." They also reported that, for both types of program, the "widening of the net" phenomenon was still in full operation. The bulk of referrals made over a five-year period were of juveniles who closely resembled "released rather than petitioned" offenders, the bulk of whom would never be arrested again, indicating that, once again, the police diversion process was concentrating upon offenders who would have been simply released in the past.

Thus, it is apparent that good intentions can lead to unintended consequences and that police diversion units may represent an extension rather than a limitation of police authority over juveniles.

CONCLUSION

The police represent the gateway to the juvenile justice system. Their job at this level is particularly difficult and subject to conflicting demands: protecting the public from crime while offering treatment and help in the best interests of the juvenile in full accordance with the constitutional rights of the youth. Efforts by the police to divert offenders have not been particularly effective in altering the scope of intervention by the juvenile justice system. It is evident that future efforts in this area should pay particular attention to the wishes of the community, social organization of the police (attitudes toward juveniles and their handling), and the "widening of the net" phenomenon, which plagues diversion programs throughout the juvenile justice system.

3

THE JUVENILE COURT:
System and Procedure

THE ORIGIN AND JURISDICTION
OF THE JUVENILE COURT

The History of the Juvenile Court

The first juvenile court in the United States came into being on July 1, 1899, in Cook County, Illinois. The court was the result of the work of individuals and organizations interested in many social causes, such as prison reform, women's suffrage, the abolition of poverty, and the welfare of children (Paulsen and Whitebread, 1974). The juvenile court was the product of increased public awareness of social problems and social justice in the nineteenth century. It was also only one of a number of social trends that sought to enhance the welfare of children, such as child labor regulation, expanding public education, and special services for disabled children (Caldwell, 1961).

The legal bases of this court were the Council of Chancery, under which the king acted as parens patriae (the father of his country) and exercised guardianship over wards of the state, and the English common-law presumption that children were more innocent than adults. These bases were used prior to the actual beginnings of the juvenile court, as part of the general child welfare movement, to establish institutions for juveniles so that they could avoid confinement in jails in New York (1825) and Boston (1826). Likewise, in the 1860s and 1870s, separate hearings for juveniles and the appointment of agents to attend juvenile hearings and protect the interests of the child were established in several jurisdictions, and from 1878 to 1898 a statewide probation system was enacted in Massachusetts as part of this movement (Caldwell, 1961).

In Chicago, welfare and civic organizations—specifically, the Chicago Woman's Club, the Catholic Visitation and Aid Society, the State Board of Charities, and the Chicago Bar Association—campaigned for the juvenile court (Caldwell, 1961). Finally, in 1899 they reached their goal. The act establishing the court called for the creation of a juvenile court in every county with a population of more than 500,000. This applied only to Cook County, so it became the first jurisdiction to have a juvenile court.

These early reformers and proponents of the juvenile court were disenchanted with the criminal court and the concept of deterrence (Besharov, 1974; Paulsen and Whitebread, 1974). They believed that the criminal court was harsh and oppressive, especially when a child was involved as the defendant, and that this punitive stance had not resulted in any reduction in crime through deterrence. In fact, the proponents felt that the treatment of children as if they had "free will" when they really were less responsible than adults unduly harmed them. They believed that the stigmas, family separation, institutionalization, and association with adult criminals only injured children, possibly creating more crime.

In lieu of the punitive concept, proponents believed that "the care, custody, and the discipline of the child should approximate as nearly as possible that which should be given by his parents" (Caldwell, 1961: 495). The objective was to find out why the child was misbehaving and then to use the information of the behavioral and medical sciences to assist the child in changing his or her ways.

The court was to have jurisdiction over children who were under the age of sixteen and found to be dependent, neglected, or delinquent. The court was to be a special jurisdiction within the circuit court, presided over by separate judges. The children were to have a separate court, separate hearings, and separate records. The procedures were to be informal, and charges were not filed against the child; instead, a petition was filed in his or her interest. Various formal components of criminal court procedure—indictments, pleadings, and juries (unless required by an interested party or judge)—were eliminated. Instead, the probation officers and the judge, through informal hearings, were to determine the causes of the problem and recommend and oversee the treatment.

The concept of the juvenile court caught on quickly. By 1920, all but three states had such courts, and by 1945, all states had courts.

Along with this geographical expansion, the jurisdiction of the juvenile court was increased in many states to include those acts in which an adult contributed to the delinquency of a child and to include the status offenses. Along with the geographic and jurisdictional growth, the court acquired a greater influence on the welfare of children, the family, and family relationships (Caldwell, 1961).

The Jurisdiction of Juvenile Court

The most common meaning of the term "jurisdiction" is the type of cases a court may hear and determine. Courts may have several types of jurisdiction: *exclusive* (no other court may hear these types of cases), *concurrent* (the right to hear the cases is shared with another court), and *original* (the court has the right to hear these types of cases for the first time).

Because juvenile courts are created by statute, their jurisdiction is also determined by statute. Juvenile courts have original jurisdiction over cases involving questions of juvenile delinquency, neglected and dependent children, children in need of supervision, and offenses committed against juveniles (Johnson, 1975). The jurisdiction is determined by both the conduct and the age of the juvenile.

Juveniles, as subjects of the juvenile court, are defined by state statute. While not all states establish a lower age limit, all have set a maximum age at which a child may be adjudicated in juvenile court (Fox, 1977). Most states set eighteen as a maximum age, though some have established seventeen and sixteen as maximum ages for jurisdiction. A juvenile, then, is an individual who is under the maximum age set for juvenile court jurisdiction (Davis, 1974). In the past, some juvenile courts had different maximum ages for males and females. This was upheld for a number of years, until *Lamb v. Brown* (1972), when the U.S. Court of Appeals for the Tenth Circuit ruled that it was unconstitutional on equal protection grounds. The court ruled that the "demonstrated facts of life," which the statute used to justify the age difference, were ambiguous, poorly defined, and "not demonstrated" as substantial. Therefore, the maximum age of jurisdiction in criminal cases involving juveniles must be the same for both males and females (Paulsen and Whitebread, 1974; Davis, 1974). In another case, *In re Patricia A.* (1972), a similar ruling was applied to maximum age differences for status offenders.

Specifically *when* maximum age for jurisdiction is determined is a crucial issue. Past state legislation was not specific. However, today most courts have established a policy of age at the time of the commission of offense as the point at which the age conditions of jurisdiction are established. As for the length of time a case may remain open, or the maximum age at which proceedings against the juvenile may be enacted, most states have no limits. However, as Fox (1977) has stated, "There would be obvious objections to a juvenile court trial for a person in his thirties, or older, even if the offense with which he is charged was committed while he was a young adolescent within the upper limits of the age jurisdiction." Therefore, some states limit the age at which proceedings may be brought against an individual. For example, the Texas Family Code says that a juvenile may have proceedings brought against him or her as long as he or she is under eighteen years of age (Fox, 1977).

In addition to the age criteria, conduct criteria are specified by statute. The types of conduct are juvenile delinquency, children in need of supervision, neglect and dependency, and offenses committed against juveniles.

Juvenile Delinquency. Most states include as acts of delinquency behaviors that violate state laws or local ordinances. These may then be acts that are crimes when performed by adults and may also include special categories of offenses applicable only to juveniles: status offenses. These may include (Fox, 1972):

(1)   habitually truant
(2)   incorrigible
(3)   beyond control of parents or guardian
(4)   growing up in idleness or crime
(5)   immoral or indecent conduct
(6)   absents self from home (without just cause) without consent
(7)   wanders streets at night, not on lawful business
(8)   smokes cigarettes (or uses tobacco in any form)
(9)   addicted to drugs
(10) uses intoxicating liquor
(11) makes indecent proposal
(12) patronizes public pool room or bucket shop
(13) attempts to marry without consent in violation of law
(14) given to sexual irregularities

Children in Need of Supervision. Because the emphasis in many areas of court jurisdiction over juveniles is upon conditions, not conduct, as is the case with many status offenses, many states separate status offenders from juvenile delinquents. Many of these states have established a special category for status offenders called "Children in need of supervision" (CHINS), "persons in need of supervision" (PINS), or "minors in need of supervision" (MINS).

Children in this category have not committed criminal acts, but have instead "misbehaved." Their behaviors, such as running away, being habitually truant, disobeying parents, or going beyond the control of parents, are believed to be symptoms of some personal or familial problem. The state must then intervene to prevent the escalation of "misbehavior" to "criminal behavior" by preventing the child from further injuring himself or herself (Besharov, 1974). Because their acts are not criminal, and because of the desire to avoid stigmatization of these children, hearings for status offenders are much more informal than are those for delinquents.

Neglect and Dependency. Because children may not receive the treatment necessary for adequate development, the juvenile court may intervene to protect the child from further injury or mistreatment (Besharov, 1974). In all but a few states, the juvenile court has this "child protective jurisdiction." The jurisdiction covers what courts refer to as cases of neglect and dependency. Most states categorize the two types of cases together; however, there is an important difference. Neglect cases involve juveniles who have been abandoned by their parents or juveniles who are neglected because their parents neglect or refuse proper treatment. Dependency, on the other hand, is the "absence of legal custodian" or inadequate care because of "physical, mental, or financial inability" (Johnson, 1975). The following are some of the instances in which the courts may intervene (Fox, 1972):

(1) when a child lacks parental care because of its parent's fault or its parent's mental or physical disability
(2) when a parent refuses or neglects to provide for a child's needs
(3) when a parent has abandoned a child
(4) when a parent refuses to provide for a child's moral and/or mental needs
(5) when a child's best interests are not being met

(6) when a child's environment, behavior, or associations are injurious to it

(7) when a child is in danger of being brought up to lead an idle, dissolute, or immoral life

(8) when a child's home, by reason of neglect, cruelty, or depravity of its parents, is unfit

While the spirit of the intent of these statutes, to ensure that children receive adequate care and treatment, is admirable, some serious concerns over these laws and the involvement of the juvenile court have been expressed.

Even though the courts have not always ruled and so agreed, many individuals express concern over the vagueness of these statutes (Johnson, 1975; Besharov, 1974; Fox, 1977). The conditions specified in many statutes, such as not meeting a child's moral or mental needs, are so vague that there is concern over the application of subjective standards that may be related to race and social class. Therefore, parents may be expected to meet conditions that are inappropriate and impossible to comply with given their race and/or social class or standard of living (Fox, 1977).

Despite these concerns, the courts have generally ruled that it is in the interest of the state to protect the rights of children and that narrowly defined statutes might detract from children's right to proper care and minimize the state's ability to protect them. Two exceptions to this were the cases of *Roe v. Conn* (1976) and *Alsager v. District Court* (1975). In the Roe case, the court ruled that an Alabama law which included as neglect a home "unfit or improper" for a child was too vague. The court ruled that the vagueness called for an official opinion of "improper," which did not necessarily mean "physical or emotional harm" and so was too open to subjective determination. Alsager resulted in a similar ruling, also stating that the statute in question was so vague that it did not inform parents of an appropriate way to act. These, however, are the exceptions to the general direction of court rulings.

Another area of concern has been that of procedural rights in cases of neglect and dependency. These are important, because the court can rule to remove the child from the home and parental care. However, "procedural rights in neglect and abuse cases have been more slow to appear than in delinquency and status offense proceedings" (Fox, 1977: 15). The trend is toward increasing the rights of parents and more formal proceedings, but most states do not provide the same procedural safeguards allowed in delinquency proceedings. Parents are allowed counsel, may be provided counsel if indigent, must be notified (unless immediate action to protect the child is necessary), and evidence must be presented to prove neglect and dependency. However, in most jurisdictions only a preponderance of evidence, and in some, clear and convincing evidence, is required to prove neglect and abuse. These standards are not as rigid as the "beyond a reasonable doubt" ruling required in cases of delinquency and adult criminal court. Some individuals believe that because the consequences can be so extreme, the parents and the child require more procedural safeguards than used in current practice.

Finally, the jurisdiction of neglect and dependency is seen by many as a burden on the juvenile court, which is already seriously overtaxed, but also, and more important, as a source of stigma for the family and an instance in which the family might be better cared for by a social service agency (Johnson, 1975). The parents of neglected and dependent children are generally people who cannot cope with life situations. Many have problems related to stress and anxiety, such as alcoholism. The formal intervention by the court may stigmatize the parents and even punish them, when what they really require is the assistance and support of a social service agency.

Offenses Committed Against Juveniles. The juvenile court may also have jurisdiction over adults when "offenses have been committed against or involving children, and also in contributing to the delinquency or dependency of the youth" (Johnson, 1975: 39). These "adult contributory" statutes vary. Sometimes the juvenile courts have exclusive jurisdiction, while at other times the jurisdiction is concurrent with criminal court. The offenses may include acts of abuse or injury, child stealing, or immoral acts or practices in front of children.

It should be apparent that the jurisdiction of this court makes it a very far-reaching and influential court. The matters that are the concern of this court are varied and complex, with the potential for extensive long- and short-term effects for youth, families, and society.

THE STRUCTURE OF JUVENILE COURT

"The juvenile justice system is not institutions, not buildings. It is not agencies. It is people making decisions on how to best handle a child and family in trouble; it is people interlocked by a process of decision, both independent and interdependent" (Besharov, 1974: 11). The heart of the juvenile justice system and the decisions of this system is the juvenile court. These are specialized courts for children which are established by state legislation. They may be part of an independent statewide court system, a special session of a lower court, or part of family court (Senna and Siegel, 1976).

Most juvenile courts are courts of general jurisdiction that have the capacity to hear juvenile cases. Only eight states have courts whose exclusive jurisdiction is limited to juvenile and family matters (Fox, 1977). Our juvenile courts, rather than being courts of specialization, are courts of "nonspecialization," according to Fox (1977). In courts of limited and special jurisdiction, only 2 percent spend more than 75 percent of their available judge time on juvenile cases, while in our courts of general jurisdiction, only 2 out of 3630 spend more than 75 percent of their time on juvenile cases. "It appears, therefore, that where authority to try juvenile cases is assigned to a court which also has jurisdiction to hear other cases, it is extremely rare that these cases occupy more than a very small percentage of the court's judicial manpower" (Fox, 1977: 10-11).

While the specific structure of the units of juvenile court may vary, the procedures performed by the court and its units and the decisions made by the court and its units are fairly constant.

The procedures performed by the court and its units are as follows:

(1) court intake: juvenile probation
    (a) screening and referral
    (b) detention decisions
    (c) predisposition case study
(2) file petition for hearing
(3) transfer proceedings
(4) adjudicatory hearing
(5) disposition hearing

Each procedure centers on a decision—that is, whether to move the child further into the formal processes and procedures of the court or to divert the child from judicial to nonjudicial procedures.

(1) *Court Intake.* Juveniles are usually referred by complaint to an intake counselor, usually part of the juvenile probation component of juvenile court. The intake unit screens the case against the juvenile and recommends a judicial or nonjudicial resolution. If a judicial solution is sought, the intake counselor determines the juvenile's status pending adjudication—that is, detention or release. The intake unit also supervises those juveniles whom its counselors place in social agencies and programs, as well as conducting a social case investigation for judges to use in determining what disposition or sentence a court established delinquent should receive.

(2) *Filing Petition for Hearing.* If the intake unit determines that a formal hearing is the best form for case resolution, the complaint/petition against the juvenile is referred to the prosecutor's office.

(3) *Transfer Proceedings.* In cases where a juvenile commits an act for which he or she may be held accountable in criminal court, most juvenile courts must conduct "waiver" proceedings to transfer the child to the jurisdiction of the criminal court.

(4) *Adjudicatory Hearing.* Once the procedures to select and use informal resolutions of a case against a child have been exhausted, an adjudicatory hearing will be held. The hearing has as its purpose the validation of the complaint levied against the child.

(5) *Dispositional Hearing.* If the court finds that the child is delinquent, neglected, dependent, or in need of supervision, then the court must determine how best to meet the needs of the child. This phase is similar to sentencing in criminal court. The outcome of these proceedings is, ideally, some form of treatment or rehabilitation, individually structured and planned in the best interests of the child. The outcome may be institutionalization, foster care placement, restitution, drug and/or alcohol rehabilitation, probation, or place-

ment in any number of public and private agencies and programs available to the court.

THE PROCEDURAL RIGHTS OF JUVENILES: AN OVERVIEW

From their beginnings in 1899 until 1966, sixty-six years, the juvenile courts operated without legal oversight or monitoring (Wadlington et al., 1983). In 1966, *Kent v. United States* became the first juvenile case to be ruled upon by the U.S. Supreme Court. This absence of attempts to oversee the procedures of the juvenile court was not surprising, since the philosophy of the juvenile court rejected legal institutions and procedures as adequate and appropriate for juvenile rehabilitation and since the federal courts had traditionally been hesitant to intervene in family matters.

However, in the 1960s increasing disenchantment and frustration with the juvenile court developed. The courts did not appear to be rehabilitating juveniles and appeared in many instances to be violating their intended purpose by "punishing under the pretense of being a social service agency, while arguing that constitutional protections were not necessary because the juvenile was being 'helped' " (Senna and Siegel, 1976).

The Kent decision laid the groundwork for the establishment of procedural safeguards for juveniles during juvenile court proceedings. In Kent, the court ruled that a youth in juvenile court had been deprived of due process while not given the promised rehabilitation. In this case, the petitioner, Kent, alleged that the juvenile court had denied due process of law in its decision to waive jurisdiction and have Kent transferred to adult criminal court. The waiver had been made without providing for a hearing. The Supreme Court, because of the serious nature of the decision to transfer jurisdiction to adult criminal court, ruled for the first time that some standards of fairness must be applied. Specifically, the court ruled that juveniles had (at least in transfer proceedings) the right to all protections implied in the Fourteenth Amendment's due process clause. With respect to the decision to waive jurisdiction, the court ruled that juveniles had the right to (1) a hearing, (2) counsel, (3) access to social services records provided to and used by the court, and (4) a statement of the facts of the full investigation and a statement of the reason a judge ruled to waive jurisdiction.

Following Kent, the *Gault* decision (1967) expanded the procedural safeguards for juveniles even further. In Gault, the Supreme Court made four very important and far-reaching decisions. The court ruled that when an adjudication of delinquency is proceeding,

(1) Notice must be given in advance of proceedings against a juvenile so that he or she has reasonable time to prepare a defense.

(2) If the proceedings may result in the institutionalization of the juvenile, then both the juvenile and the parents must be informed of their right to have counsel and be provided with one if they cannot afford to obtain one on their own.

(3) Juveniles have the protection against self-incrimination.

(4) Juveniles have the right to hear sworn testimony and to confront the witnesses against them for cross-examination.

The court was careful in both Kent and Gault to emphasize the civil nature of the proceedings, and consequently not to apply to juvenile courts the same standards that apply to adult criminal court. However, in both landmark cases the court ruled that due process did require that certain procedural safeguards be applied to at least some of the proceedings of juvenile court (Senna and Siegel, 1976) and that the important values of rehabilitation would not be undercut by these constitutional procedures (Paulsen and Whitebread, 1974).

Following the Gault and Kent decisions, the next major application of procedural safeguards came in 1970, with *In re Winship* (1970). This case questioned the use of a preponderance of evidence (as used in civil court) to establish delinquency rather than the "beyond a reasonable doubt" ruling, which applies in criminal court. The Supreme Court ruled that, in delinquency proceedings, the standard of "beyond a reasonable doubt" applied. This, then, meant that juveniles tried for crimes that are also crimes for adults had the same procedural protection as adults.

This momentum for expanding procedural safeguards was curtailed in 1971 with the Supreme Court ruling in *McKeiver v. Pennsylvania* (1971). At issue was whether juveniles tried for acts of delinquency had the right to a trial by jury. The Supreme Court ruled that there is no guarantee to the right to trial by jury for juveniles, because it would be "disruptive to the informal fact finding setting"; however, because it is not "obligatory" does not mean it is not possible (Davis, 1974).

Since the early 1970s, most revisions of juvenile court proceedings have shifted from judicial to legislative and, if they have been judicial, have occurred within specific state supreme courts. Today, the procedural rights guaranteed juveniles in court proceedings to establish delinquency are (1) advance and adequate notice of charges, (2) the right to counsel and the provision of counsel if indigent, (3) the right to confront and cross-examine witnesses, (4) the protection against self-incrimination, (5) the right to a judicial hearing with counsel prior to transfer to adult court, and (6) the right to be considered innocent until proven guilty beyond a reasonable doubt (Simonsen and Gordon, 1982).

CRITICAL ISSUE: THE TRANSFER OF JUVENILES TO ADULT CRIMINAL COURT

Prior to the inception of the juvenile court in 1899, all juveniles were tried as adults, were treated as adult criminal offenders, and, as adults, were frequently sentenced to prison. While the juvenile court and its underlying philosophy of parens patriae assumed that children should be treated differently from adults—rehabilitated and protected rather than punished—the court nonetheless recognized that certain forms of conduct should require juveniles to be tried as adults. Therefore, the juvenile court jurisdiction over a youth could be waived and the youth transferred to the jurisdiction of the adult criminal court.

Today, all jurisdictions provide, by statute, for transfer of juveniles to adult court. The underlying justifications for this procedure are (1) that the conduct presents such a danger to public safety that the juvenile must be tried as an adult, and (2) that the juvenile is not amenable to the treatment provided by the juvenile justice system and therefore should be handled by agents of the adult criminal justice system. The juvenile justice system emphasizes rehabilitation, treatment, and the avoidance of stigma for youth. However, regardless of the age of the offender, victims are injured and public safety is threatened. When the threat to the community is extreme, the retributive and punitive orientation of the criminal court is seen as more justifiable than the rehabilitative or treatment philosophy of juvenile justice (Feld, 1981). Similarly, the rehabilitative and treatment resources of the juvenile justice system are, as are all resources, finite. Some juveniles may not be amenable to the available resources and therefore "not treatable." Rather than drain the resources of juvenile justice *or* reallocate the resources so that the extensive resource expenditures required to hold and treat these more "dangerous" juveniles are not depleted, the youth can be transferred to criminal court, where the resources are available to deal with individuals who pose a serious threat to public safety (Gasper and Katkin, 1980).

As of 1983, forty-seven states and the District of Columbia permit some form of waiver in which the child may be tried in adult criminal court rather than juvenile court (Bureau of Justice Statistics, 1983). While this decision has serious implications for the child, it was not reviewed and ruled on by the U.S. Supreme Court until 1966. The landmark case in this procedure and the general procedural rights of juveniles was *Kent v. United States* (1966). In this case, the provisions of a District of Columbia statute that permitted juveniles to be transferred to criminal court after a "full investigation" was challenged. The Supreme Court ruled that this phase of processing was "critically important" due to the potential effects on the child because he or she was being tried and sentenced as an adult. Consequently, some procedural safeguards must be provided for the child. The Court then specified four procedural rights that must be provided for youth in the waiver process:

(1) the right to a hearing on the motion to waive jurisdiction of the juvenile court
(2) the right to representation by counsel in these proceedings
(3) the right of the child's counsel to have access to the records and reports used to reach a waiver decision
(4) the right to a written statement of reasons for the decision made by the court

As Senna and Siegel (1976: 229) state, this ruling was significant because "the conclusion reflects the belief that although latitude and discretion are important functions of the juvenile court system, procedures must also satisfy a fundamental fairness doctrine."

Following Kent, the state jurisdictions incorporated the Kent standards into their statutory procedures for waiver. Consequently, today most waiver proceedings require all four standards and, moreover, evidence that reasonable grounds exist to believe that the child did, in fact, commit the specified act. However, other than these broad similarities there is a great deal of variation in these waiver proceedings.

Waiver Provisions

The most prevalent form of waiver proceedings is *judicial waiver*. In almost all state jurisdictions, a juvenile judge may at his or her discretion move for or request a waiver to criminal court. Waiver proceedings may also be *legislative* in nature. That is, by state statute, offense provisions and age provisions may govern the waiver proceedings. For example, in Kentucky a child under sixteen may be transferred for capital offenses or a Class A felony, while youth sixteen and older may be transferred for any felony. While almost all states have some crime and/or age restrictions on their waiver proceedings, the restrictions are not the same. In fact, some states, such as Alaska, have no age or offense limits (Bureau of Justice Statistics, 1983).

The last form of waiver proceedings is the *prosecutor waiver*. This type of waiver, as specified in twenty-one states (Bureau of Justice Statistics, 1983), allows the prosecutor's decision concerning whether to try the juvenile in adult or criminal court to augment the existing judicial waiver statutes (Mlyniel, 1976). In another two states, Nebraska and Wyoming, the prosecutor decides whether to file in juvenile or criminal court (Bureau of Justice Statistics, 1983).

One critical issue of concern in the process of transfer is the form of the proceedings. The most prevalent form of waiver proceeding, judicial waiver, is believed to be wrought with extensive discretion (Osbun and Rode, 1984; Gasper and Katkin, 1980; Besharov, 1974). The greater the discretion, the greater the potential for abuse of that discretion. Many individuals, such as Gasper and Katkin (1980), believe that judicial discretion in waiver decisions is not sufficiently limited and consequently may be influenced unfairly by the philosophy of the judge, political pressures, or administrative convenience. For example, a judge's responses to specific crimes or his or her stance on "law and order" may influence his or her decisions about which cases to waive. Likewise, judges may be pressured by media coverage or the publicity surrounding certain crimes into making decisions that are not based on acceptable legal criteria. Last, many judges like to keep related cases in the same court. Therefore, for the sake of convenience, if one offender's case is waived to criminal court, the likelihood that a codefendant's case will be transferred may increase. These decisions can be quite inequitable and arbitrary.

The prosecutor waiver raises similar concerns. If the prosecutor is allowed great influence in this decision, then the assumption, not unlike that for judicial discretion, is that prosecutors can determine which best serves a youth, treatment or punishment (Gasper and Katkin, 1980). This assumption is problematic, given the organizational imperatives that affect prosecutors. Because of their concern with conviction rates, they may be inclined to place too much emphasis on the strength of evidence in a case and waive only those cases in which a conviction seems certain. Prosecutors, like judges, are also susceptible to political pressures (maybe even more so, since most are concerned with reelection). They may then respond more to the publicity and political pressures associated with a case than to the facts of the case.

Today, most individuals seem to agree that the use of legislative waiver proceedings is the best option in establishing procedures for juvenile transfer that are rational, just, fair, and nondiscriminatory (Feld, 1983, 1981, 1978; Besharov, 1974). The legislative procedure can set statutory guidelines and criteria that act as a control or check on judicial and prosecutional discretion. As of 1981, forty-seven states have some legislated statute that acts to limit the complete discretion of judges and prosecutions in transfer proceedings. The most frequent criterion is age, though other criteria, such as alleged offense, past record, public danger, and amenability, may also be statutory criteria for transfer decisions (Osbun and Rode, 1984). However, even legislative criteria are problematic. The legislative criteria are not consistent across jurisdictions; they may be too ambiguous truly to limit judicial discretion; the existence of these criteria cannot provide certainty of trial as an adult and may be countered by decisions concerning matters such as which crime to charge a youth with; and finally the criteria cannot necessarily predict the amenability of youth to treatment or their danger to the community (Osbun and Rode, 1984). However, the consensus seems to be that *some* legislative criteria may be better than unchecked judicial and prosecutorial discretion.

Standards for Transfer of Jurisdiction

While the consensus seems to be that *some* form of legislative standards for waiver should exist, the issue of *what* these standards should be is problematic. As mentioned earlier, the underlying justifications for transfer are (1) nonamenability to treatment and (2) threat to public safety. What criteria establish the existence of and predict further threat to public safety? What criteria show that the youth has not responded to treatment and will not respond to treatment in the future?

Since most states have some age limitations for transfer and many have some offense requirements, the assumption must be that these two criteria establish and predict nonamenability and a public safety threat. A few states use other criteria to meet the requirements of these two justifications. These include some of the following: history of delinquency, facilities available for treatment, probable cause that the youth committed the act, mental and physical condition, amenability to treatment, sophistication and maturity, need to protect society, knowing the difference between right and wrong, and accountability for acts (Paulsen and Whitebread, 1974).

In addition to the problem of which criteria show and predict nonamenability and a threat of public safety, two other, not unrelated, issues have been raised concerning standards to guide transfer decisions. First, if criteria are vague, judicial discretion will become more prominent in the decision. If judges have broad latitude to interpret criteria, they may apply criteria in different ways to different types of offenders. Similarly, if criteria are vague or nonexistent, extralegal factors may influence the decision to transfer. For example, a national survey of juvenile courts in 1975 found that severity of offense, translated to mean public safety, was the primary criterion used by 64.7 percent of the respondents as the primary justification for transfer (Gasper and Katkin, 1980). However, other studies suggest that as many as 17 percent of the judges surveyed used public sentiment toward the offense, and as many as 25 percent, the "desirability of trying the juvenile with adult co-offenders" as criteria that influenced their decision to transfer (Paulsen and Whitebread, 1974).

Second, there is much variation among criteria utilized by jurisdictions. Therefore, the probability of transfer for the same offense and offender may depend more on *where* the offense occurred and *which judge* hears the case than on objective, consistent criteria. As described in the first chapter, two juveniles who have the same characteristics and have committed the same crime may be treated quite differently by not only two different judges but also two different state jurisdictions. There is a lack of uniformity.

Feld (1983, 1981, 1978) argues that we cannot depend on current standards of clinical diagnosis and prediction to determine the amenability of treatment and danger to public safety. The research on current forms of treatment cannot tell us with any certainty what works, nor can it separate the "amenable" from the "nonamenable." Nor is there current research to suggest that clinical tests can predict future "dangerousness" or threat to public safety (Feld, 1981). The terms "amenability" and "dangerousness," Feld (1981) argues, are "standardless grants to discretion" and make the transfer process unpredictable and subjective.

Feld calls for the use of actuarial rather than clinical techniques to establish amenability and dangerousness—specifically, those offender characteristics and offense characteristics which correlate with future behavior should be considered, and legislation should be developed to exclude youth automatically on the basis of the predictive criteria from the jurisdiction of the juvenile court, therefore limiting judicial discretion. Feld (1983) suggests that current offense and past criminal record more accurately identify those who should be tried as adults than do clinical tests to determine "danger" and "amenability." However, caution must be taken to ensure that present offense is not emphasized over present offense *and* past criminal record.

Many studies of delinquency suggest that many juveniles initially arrested for serious, even violent, charges will not necessarily face repeat charges of the same type (Hamparian et al., 1978). Similarly, Wolfgang et al. (1972), in their study of delinquency in a birth cohort, found that, of those juveniles in the Philadelphia cohort with one delinquent act, 46.4 percent had no further police contact, and of those with a second violation, 34.9 percent had no further contact.

They also found that offenders with personal crimes were as likely as those with other offenses to stop after one offense (43 percent). Therefore, using only current offense does not seem to identify the truly serious, repeat offender who has not responded to the resources of criminal justice.

Past record with present offense is more justifiable and consistent with the delinquency literature. Wolfgang (1975, 1977) argues that there is a significant difference between juveniles with one or two arrests and those with five or more arrests and that, once one becomes a chronic offender, the probability of future crime is great. In fact, the data from Wolfgang's research suggest that a small number of chronic offenders account for a disproportionate number of offenses. In his study of the birth cohort, chronic offenders constituted 18 percent of the delinquents but were responsible for 52 percent of the delinquent acts. "This small but important class of youths challenges both the rehabilitatic assumptions of the juvenile court and the priority of informal, nonpunitive, and relatively short-term social control" (Feld, 1981: 499).

With these standards limiting transfer to serious, repeat offenders, judicial discretion would be minimized and the process of transfer would become more rational and predictable. Feld (1983: 497) also believes that this automatic exclusion, based on more actuarial than clinical data, would have other systemic effects:

(1) It would emphasize intervention with persistent, serious offenders and minimize the attention given to many non-serious offenders and minimize the attention given to many non-serious juvenile offenders who currently are "caught in the juvenile justice system net" when they should probably be diverted.
(2) The impetus for better representation of juveniles by their attorneys would be great. The significance of contact and adjudication in the system would be greater so attorneys would need to become more vigorous advocates to prevent their defendants from having extensive records.
(3) The system and the juvenile would be more accountable. The juvenile would be held more responsible for his/her acts. The juvenile justice system would be more accountable because criteria would be present which must be met.

While this perspective, as reflected in the research of Feld (1983, 1981, 1978), is prominent, it is not the only perspective. Gasper and

Katkin (1980) present a different and equally compelling argument for the abolition of the policy of the transfer of juveniles to adult court. These authors contend that the policy of transfer is based on a set of assumptions that are not necessarily valid. First, the transfer of a juvenile to adult court based on community danger and nonamenability to treatment assumes that the juvenile will be handled more stringently—will be punished more—in adult court than in juvenile court. However, national and state data suggest that this may not be the case. Hamparian et al., in *Youth in Adult Court: Between Two Worlds* (1982), found in a national survey that 50.5 percent of the juveniles sentenced in adult court received fines or probation, while only 11.4 percent were sentenced to jail and 30.0 percent to state adult institutions. Of those sentenced to institutions (jails and adult and juvenile facilities), the greatest portion, 26.7 percent, received a year or less, and almost half, 49.2 percent, less than three years. Similarly, in a Pennsylvania study, only 24 percent of those waived to adult court in 1977 were sentenced to adult facilities, while 23 percent were sentenced to jail and 23 percent to probation or community-based supervision (Pennsylvania Joint Council on the Criminal Justice System, 1978). While these studies did not provide comparable adult sentence data for the respective years, "an adjudicated delinquent can be confined until the end of his minority, which is typically two to six years for the 'older' delinquent" (Gasper and Katkin, 1980), not less serious than the types and lengths of sentences given in adult court.

Even if juveniles are convicted and sentenced in adult court, there is no evidence to suggest that they are less likely to recidivate than juveniles adjudicated in juvenile court. In fact, the data presented earlier on length of sentence might even suggest a lesser impact through incapacitation if juveniles are incarcerated by adult rather than juvenile court sentences.

Second, even when criteria are set, the potential for a capricious, arbitrary decision is not eliminated. Osbun and Rode (1984) studied the effect of new waiver provisions in the Minnesota statutes, which were established to provide a more objective basis for waiver decisions. The provisions set sixteen as an age criterion, as well as a combination of present offense and prior record criteria. For example, if the alleged offense was murder I, no prior record was required. If the offense was manslaughter I, the youth had to have been adjudicated delinquent for one felony offense committed in the preceding twenty-four months. Osbun and Rode found that even after these provisions were in place, almost two-thirds of the youth whom prosecutors sought to transfer did not meet the criteria and that only 45.5 percent of those actually transferred met the criteria. In assessing the differences between those who met the criteria and those who were actually transferred, Osbun and Rode (1984: 198) found that the criteria were too simplistic and rigid, which resulted in the singling out of too many youth as potentials for transfer: "The data indicate that the presumptive criteria identify a large subgroup of juveniles who do not on closer examination appear to be very serious offenders." They were usually property offenders with no history of violence, with short delinquent histories and few prior contacts with the juvenile justice system. Therefore, the objective criteria fared no better than the discretionary decisions of prosecutors and judges. In fact, Osbun and Rode argue that discretion may be the better mechanism, since it allows a closer look at the details and qualitative characteristics of the delinquent career of a youth.

The solution? According to Gasper and Katkin (1980), abolition of the ability to transfer a child to criminal court would force a renovation of the entire juvenile justice system. Resources would be reallocated to deal with serious juveniles, and many minor, nonserious offenders, who should be diverted, would thus be forced from the system.

What this would mean for the juvenile justice system as it reorganized to address solely serious juvenile crime is unclear. Gasper and Katkin (1980) suggest that it would necessarily retain its treatment orientation, since the justifications for treatment—that delinquency is the product of social conditions, that juvenile crime is a "cry for help," and that there is an obligation to "help" rather than punish youth—have not been disproved or weakened. However, the juvenile court might as easily become a court more similar to adult criminal court and incorporate more of a "just deserts" model, along with the rights and privileges afforded adult criminal defendants. If this were the case, the next logical question to be raised would be: Why have a juvenile court at all?

4

THE ADJUDICATION PROCESS

DETENTION

When a child is taken into custody by a police officer, the officer has several required and optional actions to take. Most jurisdictions specify these by statute (Paulsen and Whitebread, 1974):

(1) Police must notify parents or concerned persons that the child has been taken into custody.
(2) Police may release the child to parents, guardians, or custodians with an appropriate warning.
(3) Police may initiate court action and release the child to the parents upon a promise to return the child to court unless shelter care or detention is required.
(4) Police may take the child to the intake unit or to a detention or shelter care facility designated by the court or to a medical facility if they believe the child is suffering from a physical condition requiring prompt treatment or diagnosis for "evidentiary" reasons.
(5) If the child is taken into custody, prompt written notice of custody and the reasons for custody must be given to the parents, guardian, or custodian and to the court.

If the juvenile is taken to the intake unit, agents in this unit investigate the case and make initial detention or release decisions. If the child has been placed in detention by a police officer, probation officers in the intake unit must assess the case immediately and determine whether to continue detention or release the child (Eldefonso and Coffey, 1976).

In most instances, juvenile court statutes require the release of the child within forty-eight hours unless a petition for a court hearing has been filed. Likewise, most states provide for a detention hearing and are increasingly giving juveniles the right to counsel and to hear and confront witnesses during this hearing (Besharov, 1974; Eldefonso and Coffey, 1976).

Detention following arrest is considered justifiable for more reasons when the arrestee is a juvenile than when the arrestee is an adult. While all states do not provide statutory criteria to make the detention decision, the usual justifications are (1) a threat to public safety due to the severity of the crime and/or the probability of committing another crime, (2) the parents are not cooperative and may not return the child to court for the hearing, (3) the home conditions make it necessary because there is no responsible adult able or willing to supervise and care for the child, (4) injury or harm may come to the child (for example, he or she may run away again or may be injured by others), (5) the child may not return to court (he or she may run away), and (6) the child is beyond the control of the parents (Rubin, 1977; Johnson, 1985). Unlike an adult, the juvenile may be detained pending adjudication solely for his or her own protection (Senna and Siegel, 1976).

Like the criteria for detention prior to adjudication, the right to bail is not the same for juveniles and adults. Bail for juveniles is not considered to be a constitutional right. In 1968, the U.S. Supreme Court heard the case of *In re Whittington*, in which the question of the federal constitutional right to bail for juveniles was raised. The court did not rule for or against this right. Therefore, about half of the states provide for the use of bail with juveniles. In some states, the right to bail is statutory; in others, it can be used as a discretionary release option (Besharov, 1974; Rubin, 1979). A few states prohibit the use of bail (Besharov, 1974; Simonsen and Gordon, 1982).

The issue of bail is complex. Placement in detention pending adjudication is important as an indication of how the court will view the child in later proceedings. If a child is detained pending adjudication, then the court may be more inclined to recommend institutionalization if the child is found to be delinquent (Besharov, 1974). Juveniles may also be detained in some states without probable cause, which is determined at their preliminary hearing (Rubin, 1979). Additionally, in many jurisdictions there may be no separate facility for juveniles, so they are to be housed separately from adults, but this may not be possible if jails are crowded or facilities to house juveniles separately are not available. The general theme of those who would support bail for juveniles is that the reality of the conditions of confinement, the effects of confinement, and the criteria for confinement justify the right to bail.

Those who oppose this right do so on philosophical as well as practical grounds. They believe that the philosophy of the juvenile justice system promotes the generous use of release to parents and that the state is therefore responsible for detaining "problem" children. Since most get released to parents, bail is not required. More practical concerns are: (1) Where would the juvenile get the money for bail? (2) Would a bail bondsman provide money to a juvenile when his or her parents could not or would not provide it? (3) What, if any, responsibility would the juvenile feel toward those individuals who put up the bail money? (4) Would bail not make release overly dependent on economics, as it is in the adult court? (Simonsen and Gordon, 1982).

The fact of the matter is that, despite efforts to release most juveniles, many must be detained in detention facilities or jails because there is no one to whom they can be released. In 1982, 76 percent of the juveniles detained in adult jails were awaiting adjudication, while only 57 percent of all adults who were detained were awaiting trials (Bureau of Justice Statistics, 1982a). In the same year, 45,351 juveniles were held in public juvenile facilities on any given day. Of these, 11,917, or 26 percent, were awaiting adjudication. Data on the crime of these juveniles were available on only 8,593. Among those for whom data were available, only 37 percent were alleged to have committed "more serious" violent or property crimes, 2 percent alcohol-related crimes, 5.5 percent drug-related crimes, and 8.6 percent public order crimes. Whether we are in fact detaining the "problem" juveniles is questionable. Likewise, whether we can detain juveniles in adult jails given the conditions of these jails, especially at a rate of pretrial detention that is higher than that for adults, is also questionable. However, given that parents must, in the end, be responsible for juveniles released into their custody, would parents who refuse to accept release of their children post bond for the same juvenile? Could parents or other family members or legal guardians or custodians afford to post bond, given the economic status of the families of most juveniles who are placed in detention? It is not an easy issue to decide. However, making bail available would seem reasonable even if, for some juveniles, the realization of release became an economic issue. We have had no difficulty accepting this fact in adult court.

WHO IS DETAINED AND WHY?

In 1982, over a half-million juveniles were admitted to public juvenile detention facilities nationwide. This represents a 17 percent decrease in admissions since 1974 (Office of Juvenile Justice and Delinquency Prevention, 1983). However, the average daily number of residents was up from 46,753 in 1974 to 50,399 in 1982. Of those juveniles held in public facilities, 27 percent were held pending resolution of their case. The average length of time spent in pretrial detention was fifteen days. These numbers of juveniles housed in detention facilities represent a rate of 184 per 100,000 juveniles within the potential jurisdiction of juvenile court. This is an increase from the 1979 rate of 167 per 100,000 eligible population. During this time period, twenty-seven states reported an increased rate of detention. Since the percentage of juveniles committed versus juveniles awaiting adjudication has remained constant for this period, 27 percent, it would appear that nationally we are holding more juveniles in both pretrial and long-term detention.

In 1982, approximately 300,000 juveniles were admitted to jails, approximately 74 percent of whom on any given day were awaiting a preliminary hearing of adjudication (Bureau of Justice Statistics, 1982b). In most instances, these juveniles were held in jail because there were no separate juvenile detention facilities. In nineteen states, statutory provisions require segregation from adults in jails, but these provisions are frequently violated (Simonsen and Gordon, 1982). Juveniles are also housed in private facilities. The average daily population of private facilities in 1979 was 28,678 juveniles. Approximately 3 percent were awaiting adjudication (Bureau of Justice Statistics, 1983).

Therefore, on any given day, more than 15,000 juveniles are held in custody while they await resolution of their cases. These juveniles are most often male, fifteen years of age, white, and held pending resolution of a delinquency charge (Bureau of Justice Statistics, 1983, 1982b; Office of Juvenile Justice and Delinquency Prevention, 1983). However, when population representation is taken into consideration, blacks in detention account for 2.5 times the share of blacks in the general population aged ten to seventeen (Office of Juvenile Justice and Delinquency Prevention, 1983).

While it is hard to obtain national data on the characteristics of only pretrial or preadjudication detainees, several studies suggest some trends. In 1971, a National Council of Crime and Delinquency survey in upstate New York found that 43 percent of the juveniles held in jail were "persons in need of supervision" (PINS) who had no felony or misdemeanor charge and were held solely because no detention facilities were available (in Sarri, 1974). Several other studies suggest that status offenders are frequently held despite the recent efforts to reduce this procedure. Pawlak (1972) found the detention rate of status offenders lower than that of violent offenders but greater than that of property offenders. Similarly, Cohen (1975b) and Pawlak (1977) found that many repeat status offenders were often detained as frequently as juveniles alleged to be delinquent. These and other studies have also found the probability of detention for status offenders to be related to the gender of the juvenile. For example, Velimesis (1969), Pawlak (1972, 1977), Sarri (1974), and Chesney-Lind (1977) reported that females are more likely than males to be held for status offenses. Chesney-Lind (1977) reported that female status offenders were three times as likely to be held as male status offenders.

Fenwick (1982), in a study of a court in a large eastern city, found that family affiliation was the sole determinant of detention. Sex, age, and race had no effect. Likewise, legal factors such as seriousness of offense were not significant influences. Instead, the juvenile's integration into his or her family unit was the most significant factor. Family disaffiliation may be seen by court personnel as a factor that is a "predelinquent" condition, so they do not want to return the child to the situation. It may also be viewed as a source of delinquency in that the controls or control potential over the juvenile is not utilized.

In either case, intake workers appeared to detain children whose parents exhibited little interest, who came from broken homes, and who engaged in few family activities and had poor family relationships. While the strength of this variable is surprising, its influence is not inconsistent with the family orientation of the juvenile court.

Minority and lower-class offenders have higher rates of detention (Cohen, 1975a; Sarri, 1974; Sumner, 1971; Pawlack, 1977). However, the difference is not extreme. Empey (1982) discusses several reasons for this. First, higher rates of arrest and victimization among lower-class and minority youth would explain their higher rates of detention. However, if white, middle-class, especially female, youth are discriminated against for status offenses, the difference would be minimized. A second tendency may also explain this finding, which is "contrary to expectation." Officials may act to confine higher-status youth in an effort to teach them a lesson. The officials may be more concerned about the morality of higher-status youth than the morality of lower-status juveniles. "Detention has been viewed as a desirable way of disciplining those whom officials have considered worth saving" (Empey, 1982: 346).

Even though most statutes justify detention because of (1) the danger of flight, (2) danger of harm to self and others, and (3) poor home conditions, other extralegal factors have been found to influence the detention decision. Those influences are (Sarri, 1974):

(1) Location of the unit: The further away it is from the jurisdiction the less likely it is to be utilized.
(2) Time of apprehension: Juveniles apprehended during office hours are more likely to be detained than those apprehended during nonoffice hours.
(3) Where apprehended: Juveniles who are apprehended in settings where parents are not present or are less likely to be present and therefore intervene are more likely to be detained.
(4) Availability of intake: When an intake officer is available to screen the youth immediately, the juvenile is less likely to be detained.
(5) Credibility of referral source: The more credible the source, the more probable the detention.
(6) Court's perception of detention: When the court sees detention as in the community's interest, detention is more likely. Therefore, public

attitudes toward detention, the offense, and the juvenile are deter-
minants. Likewise, the nature of court relations with the public is
important.

Despite efforts to change detention policies and procedures, all too
many children are placed in detention facilities. P. M. Wald (1976:
119-120) summarized the problem most succinctly:

> For years, critics of our juvenile court system have deplored the
> horrors of juvenile detention before trial. The statistics are dreary:
> over half a million juveniles annually detained in "junior jails,"another
> several hundred thousand held in adult jails, penned like cattle,
> demoralized by lack of activities and trained staff, often brutalized.
> Over half the facitilies in which juveniles are held have no psychiatric
> or social work staff. A fourth have no school program. The median age
> of detainees is fourteen; the novice may be sodomized within a matter
> of hours. Many have not been charged with a crime at all. From New
> York to California, the field reports repeat themselves depressingly.
>
> Generally critics agree about where the fault lies and what ought to be
> done. They have scored the police, intake officers at the juvenile court,
> and the courts themselves. They have shown that too little money is
> spent on recruiting and training good staff and on mounting con-
> structive programs in detention facilities. They have called for
> alternatives to detention for juveniles who "can't go home again" but
> are not really dangerous to anyone. Still, progress is painfully slow.
> While several of our larger cities report that fewer juveniles are being
> detained before trial than in previous years, in other cities overall
> estimates continue to grow. When a situation as unsavory as juvenile
> detention persists as long as it has, reappraisal is essential. Any new
> look at the problem requires an assessment of what has been done or
> attempted in the past.

What are the options? More stringent legislative guidelines to
control and minimize the use of detention, and more options for
children who cannot be returned to their home but should not and
need not be detained for public safety considerations. For example,
Young and Pappenfort (1977) surveyed fourteen detention alternative
programs. These consisted of home detention, "attention homes,"

runaway centers, and private foster homes. The study found these alternatives "about equal in their ability to keep those youth for whom the programs were designed trouble free and available to court." Most reported a rate for offense pending adjudication of less than 5 percent. The researchers also felt that more children could have been placed in these facilities had the courts not been so hesitant to use them.

As reported by Rubin (1977), the Institute of Judicial Administration American Bar Association Juvenile Justice Standards Project suggested limiting detention to juveniles (1) charged with felony offenses that resulted in bodily harm or threat of harm to others, (2) charged with offenses that, if proven, would result in commitment to a secure institution, (3) who had committed an offense while on probation or parole, or pending court action, (4) who had escaped from an institution or placement following adjudication, or (5) who had a recent record of voluntary failure to appear.

These same standards stated that detention should never be used to punish the juvenile; to allow parents to avoid legal responsibilities; to satisfy the victim, community, or police; to permit more convenient access to juveniles; or because alternative options do not exist.

More options and standards to limit the use of detention can also save money. For example, home detention in St. Louis in 1971 cost $4.85 per day, compared to $17.54 per day for detention in a juvenile facility (Rubin, 1977). In 1982, the annual operating cost for public juvenile detention facilities was $21,926.00 per resident. Since group homes, home detention, and other options should be less costly, more potential placements could be developed. Moreover, even if they require costs equal to detention facilities, which they should not, the potential harm to the child that would be avoided could justify the cost.

THE ADJUDICATORY HEARING

The proceedings against a juvenile begin with the filing of a petition against or on behalf of the child which alleges that he or she is delinquent, in need of supervision, neglected, or dependent. This petition is like a complaint filed against an adult in criminal court. The petition may be filed by police officers, probation officers, victims, or other interested parties.

The petition serves two functions. First, it details the charges or allegations to the court and so defines why the court has jurisdiction and the options and actions available to the court. Second, it informs the juvenile and his or her family of the allegations being made so that the appropriate defense may be prepared (Besharov, 1974). With the filing of a petition, a hearing date is set and notice must be given.

According to the *Gault* decision (1967) juveniles have the right to (1) timely notice and (2) notice that is adequate to advise the juvenile and his or her parents of the allegations of misconduct. Most states have set time limits for notice to be provided. If the summons to court is delivered personally, most states require that it be delivered at least twenty-four hours before the hearing. If it is delivered by mail, most states require delivery at least five days before the hearing date (Wadlington et al., 1983). In some jurisdictions, the summons to appear in court serves as notice; in others, a copy of the petition accompanies the summons (Besharov, 1974). This timely and adequate notice is important because if the adversary system is to operate appropriately, each side (defense and prosecution) must know a great deal about the other's case so that each can adequately test the legitimacy of the opposing case in court. The mechanism for finding out about the facts supporting an allegation is called *discovery*. The *Kent* decision (1966) "represents the logical beginning point of any study of judicial treatment of discovery in juvenile proceedings" (Wadlington et al., 1983: 444). In Kent, the Supreme Court ruled that the defense counsel had the right to access to social service records used to make the waiver decision. While there has since been some "liberalization" of discovery limitations in juvenile proceedings, the lower courts have not held that juveniles have a constitutional right to discovery. Instead, discovery limits are generally imposed by judicial and legislative rule-making. Consequently, judges may determine the justification for discovery on a case-by-case basis. In most instances, states only provide statutory provisions which give counsel access to social service and other court records. Some scholars and practitioners believe that this is appropriate, given the less formal nature of juvenile proceedings. However, others contend that it is sometimes hard for counsel to determine the exact nature of the case against his of her client and that "surprise weakens the fact-finding process since a person cannot challenge the unknown" (Paulsen and Whitebread, 1974: 153).

Once the petition has been filed and notice given, the juvenile is arraigned. The function of this early hearing in court is multiple: (1) The juvenile is advised of his or her legal rights, (2) the judge asks how he or she will plea, (3) the judge determines whether the defendant wants counsel or requires appointed counsel if indigent, (4) in some instances, the petition may be reviewed by the judge to determine if a case exists with enough merit to follow through, (5) the judge may issue summons for witnesses or warrants for an absent part, (6) detention decisions and medical or psychological exam requests may be made, and (7) a date for trial or next appearance will be set (Besharov, 1974).

Once the juvenile has been arraigned, various pretrial hearings may be set to establish such things as the existence of "probable cause" to believe the juvenile committed the crime. These are usually informal and follow relaxed evidentiary rules. If the case is not diverted, dismissed, or decided at one of these early stages, the next step in the process is the actual adjudicatory hearing.

The adjudicatory hearing is a fact-finding hearing. The purpose of this hearing is to hear evidence on the allegations made in the petition and to determine from the evidence whether the child committed the delinquent acts, the acts which suggest that he or she is in need of supervision, or whether the child is in fact neglected or dependent. The early procedures of juvenile court did not adhere to the same procedures of adult criminal court. The juvenile court was to be a "service-oriented, nonadversarial" court which functioned to "treat and diagnose" children (Senna and Siegel, 1976). Therefore, the court should not be bound by the formal procedures of criminal court.

ADJUDICATORY RIGHTS

The court's inability to rehabilitate and failure to provide constitutional safeguards came under increasing criticism. "Juvenile courts apparently were punishing many children under the pretense of being a social-service agency, while arguing that constitutional protections were not necessary because the juvenile was being 'helped' in the name of the 'state' " (Senna and Siegel, 1976: 267). The U.S. Supreme Court began changing this situation through a formalization of fact-finding procedures in 1966 with the *Kent* case. This case provided procedural safeguards during the waiver hearings for transfer of juveniles to adult court.

Following the Kent decision, *In re Gault* (1967) further expanded these procedural safeguards. The Gault decision for the first time called for the application of the "concept of fundamental" fairness to juvenile proceedings. This meant that the due process clause of the Fourteenth Amendment was applied and certain procedural guaranties introjected into the adjudication of delinquency cases. Under Gault, a delinquency case was one that involved the alleged commission of a criminal statute and that might, if established, result in the commitment of the juvenile to an institution. Because of the gravity of the consequences, the Supreme Court ruled that the juvenile had the rights (1) to fair and adequate notice, (2) to representation by counsel, (3) to confront and cross-examine witnesses, and (4) against self-incrimination.

The Gault decision introduced dramatic changes in the juvenile justice system. The requirement of these rights was technically limited, in this case, to the adjudicatory stage. However, it promoted major legal reform systemwide such that today many of these rights are applied at all stages of processing.

The Right to Counsel

The right to counsel has been interpreted in various ways by the state jurisdictions. As stated earlier, the ruling technically applied only to juveniles alleged to be delinquents who faced potential commitment. Gault did not mention instances involving "persons in need of supervision" (PINS—alleged status offenders), nor did it mention stages other than adjudication, such as intake or detention hearings. Consequently, some states entitle juveniles to counsel "at all stages of the proceedings" (Wadlington et al., 1983). Some extend the right to counsel to PINS because a finding in this instance can result in commitment (Paulsen and Whitebread, 1974). Others extend the right to counsel to neglect and dependency cases as well (Simonsen and Gordon, 1982).

In instances in which the right to counsel is present, juveniles have the related right to public appointed counsel if they are indigent. The youth also have the right to elect to waive counsel if they so desire. However, this ability to do so responsibly may be questioned. In these instances, an attorney will usually consult with the family before this right is waived and the waiver is accepted (Simonsen and Gordon, 1982).

The Right Against Self-Incrimination

Several important provisions are related to the right against self-incrimination as provided by Gault. Generally, confessions alone, when not presented in court, are not considered sufficient for adjudication. While some states provide for this right by statute, others do not. In all cases, if a confession in court is accepted, the assumption is that the juvenile has been informed of his or her right not to confess.

Related to this, social reports compiled by probation officers during intake and detention proceedings cannot be used at the adjudicatory hearing. Neither can judges view these reports prior to the hearing. Lastly, cousel has the right to see these, or other, social reports, which may be used by the court at disposition hearings or in neglect proceedings (Paulsen and Whitebread, 1974).

The Right to Confront and
Cross-Examine Witnesses

Some jurisdictions permit the use of hearsay in delinquency proceedings. The Supreme Court has ruled that hearsay is not a direct violation of the right to confront and cross-examine witnesses if the hearsay is permitted for "salient and cogent" reasons. However, if it is not admitted as an exception to the general hearsay rule, which allows people to testify about only those facts they have direct knowledge of without establishing its significance, the courts have not found its use acceptable (Davis, 1974).

Other related issues are the right to be present at the hearing and the acceptability of accomplice confessions. Some states specify by statute that the child has the right to be present. Others provide for this right but allow for its waiver except in delinquency proceedings. The acceptability of accomplice confessions cannot, in most states, be the sole basis for conviction. It must be supported by other evidence that links the defendant with the crime. In both instances, an attempt is made, through court procedures, to determine that witness testimony is as fair and accurate as it can be. These are the objectives underlying the right against self-incrimination.

Other Adjudicatory Rights

Following the Gault decision, the Supreme Court continued to legalize the juvenile justice process. In 1970, in the decision for *In re Winship* (1970), the Court established a standard of proof in delinquency cases comparable to the standard used in adult courts. Specifically, "beyond a reasonable doubt" became the standard of proof in delinquency cases. This meant that the delinquency of a juvenile must be established with "no substantial uncertainty" of guilt. The court ruled that this more stringent standard was required because of the loss of liberty that could result from a finding of delinquency.

Some states have adopted a narrow interpretation of this ruling and so require proof beyond a reasonable doubt only for cases of delinquency. Other standards, such as "clear and convincing" evidence, then apply in cases involving status offenders. Other states have adopted a broad interpretation of the ruling and require proof beyond a reasonable doubt for both delinquency and status offense cases.

This momentum toward legalization was curtailed with the ruling of the Supreme Court in *McKeiver v. Pennsylvania* (1971). In this case, the Court was asked to rule on the constitutional right of juveniles to a trial by jury. The Court believed that a jury trial would introduce too much change into the character of juvenile court. The traditional delays, formalities, and publicity would alter the character of the Court, and it would be no different from adult criminal court (Paulsen and Whitebread, 1974). As a result of the ruling, most states do not provide juveniles the right to a trial by jury. The ruling, however, did not prohibit juveniles from trial by jury. Therefore, a number of states provide for jury trials in some instances by statute or judicial decision (Wadlington et al., 1983).

Two related rights are the right to public trial and the right to a speedy trial. Because of the less formal nature of the proceedings and an attempt to protect the child, the right to a public trial is not guaranteed. However, some states, such as Alaska, will allow juveniles to have public trials if they request this form of hearing. The right to a speedy trial is applicable to juveniles, and most states grant this right by statute if the juvenile is detained pending a hearing. As is the case in adult court, an attempt is made to minimize pretrial detention because the conditions of confinement constitute punishment without the required finding of guilty.

THE DISPOSITION HEARING

One of the most significant components of the juvenile justice process is the disposition hearing. This hearing follows the adjudicatory hearing and is comparable to a sentencing hearing in adult criminal court. The outcome of this hearing is some determination of the consequences that are to follow from a finding of delinquent, in need of supervision, or neglected or dependent at the adjudicatory hearing. This determination is one of the "critically important" stages of processing mentioned in *Kent* (1966). Because of this, most states, by statute or matter of practice, require a disposition hearing that is separate from the adjudicatory hearing (Paulsen and Whitebread, 1974).

The determination of the disposition of a child is, ideally, based on rehabilitative ideals. Specifically, the needs of the offender are assessed, the best programs to meet these individual needs are identified, and the child is required to pursue the rehabilitative requirements established by the court. Ideally the disposition is tied not only to conduct but also to the needs of the child. Likewise, the disposition is not determinate. Instead, termination of the program for rehabilitation is based on individual change and rehabilitation.

These ideals have changed and the goals of general and specific deterrence substituted for rehabilitation. Consequently, the courts in reality concentrate more on conduct and dispositions proportionate to conduct than on the specialized needs of the child (Wadlington et al., 1983).

The disposition hearing is less formal than the adjudicatory hearing and so operates on more informal rules of evidence and procedure. Juveniles have the right to counsel and the right to hear and present evidence. However, judges may consider evidence at this hearing which is considered inadmissible at the adjudicatory hearing. These relaxed rules are allowed in an effort to make the "wisest and fairest" decision, taking into account the needs of the child, public interests, and available resources.

The key to determining the individualized treatment is the social report. This report is not admissible in the adjudicatory hearing but is central to the disposition determination. The objective of the report is to develop a complete understanding of the juvenile and his or her family to determine the appropriate program for rehabilitation and treatment (Besharov, 1974). The report is compiled after a pre-disposition investigation has been conducted. This investigation is performed by individuals from the probation department and includes interviews with the juvenile, family members, school officials, and possibly social service and/or mental health officials agencies with which the child or his or her family has been involved. Various records, such as school, mental health, past delinquency, and physical health records, are also reviewed. The report then contains information pertaining to the following (Rubin, 1979):

—present offense

—child's statement concerning the offense

—family relationships

—school report

—detention report if detained pending resolution

—social service or mental health agencies that served the child or family

—physical health

The report also contains a recommendation from the probation officer to the judge on the appropriate disposition. The judge is not obligated to follow this recommendation but usually concurs, as reported in Rubin (1977) who found that judges agreed with probation officers in 76 percent of the cases.

While the social report should be as detailed as possible to facilitate individualized justice through rehabilitation, the fact is that many times the report contains only "critical facts" (Besharov, 1974). Too many times, caseworkers are overburdened and unable to collect the type of comprehensive information required in theory. Therefore, a social report may contain only the most obvious and available information on the child and not enough to make a detailed determination of the child's needs and how best to meet them.

After the judge has had time to examine the social report and the recommendation of the probation officer, the judge determines the disposition of the juvenile. The judge has a great deal of discretion in determining the type of disposition. Judges may elect to:

(1) Dismiss the case unconditionally—reject the court's jurisdiction over the juvenile. This must be done if the allegations are not proven.
(2) Suspend judgment: The judge can postpone the decision with certain conditions which, if met, will allow the juvenile to avoid a more stringent disposition; for example, if a juvenile agrees to return to school and remain enrolled, the judge will suspend further action against the child.
(3) Issue an order of protection: If parental behavior is determined to contribute to the child's problems, the judge may order parents to change their behavior and/or treatment of the child.
(4) Order probation—give the child a conditional release under the formal supervision of juvenile court probation or other court agency.
(5) Order placement, commitment, or institutionalization in a public or private facility.

In 1979, those cases for which a petition was filed in juvenile court resulted most often (47.0 percent) in a disposition decision to place the juvenile on probation. Twenty-four percent of the cases were dismissed, 1.4 percent were referred to adult criminal court, 4.8

percent of the juveniles were referred to public or private agencies, 10.4 percent were referred to institutions, and 12.3 percent of the cases received other varied forms of disposition (National Center for Juvenile Justice, 1982).

Precisely what determines the eventual disposition decision is a set of varied, complex, and often interrelated factors. Paulsen and Whitebread (1974) identified the following factors as influential in judicial decision making that would determine the disposition of a child in juvenile court:

(1) *The personal values and philosophy of the judge.* Juvenile court judges are people. They have values and beliefs that direct their responses to behaviors, as we all do. Judges who are especially concerned about violent crime may respond more severely to these offenses. Judges who believe in community treatment may be more inclined to use probation. In any case, no matter how objective a judge tries to be, these personal values and philosophies will influence his or her professional decisions.

(2) *The nature of the offense and its characteristics, such as the extent of harm done, may also influence the final disposition decision.* Judges respond more harshly to offenses that cause more harm, especially those involving personal injury.

(3) *The past record of the juvenile also influences the disposition outcome.* Juvenile judges operate under an "educational model." Judges want to "teach the child a lesson" and through the "lesson" change the child's behavior. The judges are then more inclined to be lenient the first time a child comes before the court and to increase the serverity of the disposition upon subsequent returns to court.

(4) *Juvenile judges may also take into account psychological causes or contributors to behavior, especially if they accept the medical model of behavior.* They tailor the court disposition to meet the child's need for psychological treatment.

(5) *Experience may also affect the disposition decision.* While judges and probation officers generally agree, less experienced judges are more inclined to agree with probation officers than are experienced judges. It may be that with experience comes the confidence to be able to make a disposition decision that is not consistent with the recommendations of other court personnel.

(6) *The attitude of the child and the child's parents as well as evidence of parental control and responsibility also influence the disposition decision.* For example, a suspended judgment is a more probable disposition outcome if the child and parents impress the judge with their willingness and ability to meet conditions. An order of protection may not be possible if parents are hostile and noncompliant. Similarly, if parents are unable to control the child, institutionalization or placement of the child in a foster home, group home, or other supervision setting may be the only option.

(7) *The availability of treatment and rehabilitative facilities and services as well as the costs of these services also influences the outcome of a disposition decision.* Lack of space in juvenile institutions, limited public mental health or substance abuse services and facilities, overburdened foster care homes, and the expense to the state and individual of services and placement options may help determine a judge's decision. A judge may, for example, not be able to use foster care for a child if no openings exist in foster homes. Similarly, a judge may not be able to require that a juvenile undergo specific psychological treatment if that treatment is not available through public or welfare facilities and the juvenile cannot afford the cost of private treatment. Many judges may also be inclined to use probation rather than institutionalization because of the higher costs of the latter to taxpayers.

(8) *Politics may also influence the decisions of juvenile judges.* These judges must respond to a public and must, especially if they are in elected positions, respond to public demands. As the public's response to juvenile delinquency or forms of juvenile delinquency changes, the decisions of judges may also change. For example, as the public becomes less tolerant of juvenile crime and especially serious juvenile crime, judges will become more harsh in their disposition of serious juvenile offenders.

While all of these factors may come into play, probably the most significant influence is the availability of alternatives for disposition. Most juvenile judges generally agree that it is preferable to place the child back in the home or at least to maintain the child in the community. However, if the home is inappropriate and community treatment options are not available, institutionalization becomes the only viable option. Therefore, community resources to create and maintain alternatives to incarceration are critical (Rubin, 1977).

The concern with judicial decision making is reflected in studies that attempt to determine what offender and offense characteristics are related to the disposition outcome. These studies have concentrated primarily on five factors; severity of offense, prior court referrals and offenses, sex, socioeconomic status, and race of the offender. The findings of these studies are at present inconclusive yet still worth mention. These studies attempt to measure the relationship between the variables mentioned earlier and severity of disposition. In each case, community treatment in some form was considered less severe than institutionalization.

Race, Gender, and Socioeconomic Status

In some instances, a relationship between race and incarceration has been established (Terry, 1967; Arnold, 1971; Thornberry, 1973; Cohen, 1975b). In some studies, this relationship was found to be based not on the race of the offender but on severity of offense and past delinquency record. The relationship between race and disposition existed because race of the offender was related to offense severity and delinquency record. When the researchers controlled for the effects of offense severity and past offense history, the relationship between race and incarceration was not evident (Terry, 1967; Cohen, 1975). However, in other studies the results suggest that even when offense severity and delinquent history are controlled, blacks are institutionalized at a higher rate than whites (Thornberry, 1973). Therefore, some authors, such as Arnold (1971), argue that there is bias and discrimination in operation.

The status of findings related to the socioeconomic status of the offender is similar. The findings are inconclusive. Some suggest that lower socioeconomic offenders are more likely to be incarcerated (Thornberry, 1973), while others find that this relationship disappears when severity of offense and prior record are taken into consideration (Terry, 1967).

Studies that seek to assess the impact of the gender of the offender are similarly inconclusive. Overall, males have a higher rate of incarceration than females. However, in some instances females are more likely to be incarcerated for status offenses and to receive longer sentences for status offenses than males (Lerman, 1979; Chesney-Lind, 1982; Huntington, 1982; Grimes, 1983). In fact, 75 percent of all juvenile females are arrested and incarcerated for status offenses (Huntington, 1982). These authors argue that a double standard exists for the two gender groups. Females are seen as more "vulnerable to abuse and exploitation" and so in need of greater protection. They are also expected to adhere to "stricter standards of acceptable behavior" (Grimes, 1983). Consequently, females who defy parental authority and/or violate sexual norms are more likely to be "retained in the system" for their own protection (Chesney-Lind, 1982), while males who commit similar acts are filtered out.

The variations in these findings are not surprising. The studies were conducted at different times in different jurisdictions. It is possible, however, to conclude that in some jurisdictions bias and discrimination against certain individuals does exist. It is not evident that it exists systemwide in juvenile justice; instead, it varies from court to court (Cohen, 1975b).

CRITICAL ISSUE:
DECRIMINALIZING STATUS OFFENSES

As Wadlington et al. (1983: 602) have stated, "Legal sanctions against noncriminal misbehavior by children predate the juvenile court movement." There has always been concern over the misbehavior of children and the failure of the family to instill appropriate values, beliefs, and controls. Consequently, with the development of juvenile justice and its concept of parens patriae, the misbehavior as well as criminal behavior of juveniles became a logical area of jurisdiction.

Beginning in the early 1960s, however, there have been "increasing calls for limiting the use of the juvenile justice system to control troublesome behavior by youth" (LaTessa et al., 1984: 145). These suggestions to limit juvenile court involvement in status offenses have specifically called for the decriminalization of status offenses and

deinstitutionalization and diversion of status offenders. This movement has been generated by the belief that the court has been
ineffective in solving the problems of status offenders, has been
unjust in its treatment of these offenders, and has, through labeling
and stigmatization, created more problems and increased criminality
among these youth (LaTessa et al., 1984).

Since the 1960's, various attempts have been made to limit the
state's authority over status offenders. However, the extent to which
this has been accomplished is questionable, as is the utility of
continued support of the current practices.

In the late 1960s and early 1970s, 25 percent of all court
adjudications involved status offenders (President's Commission on
Law Enforcement and the Administration of Justice, 1967). By 1980,
the percentage had decreased only slightly. In this year, 19.7 percent
of all referrals were for status offenses (Bureau of Justice Statistics,
1983). This was in spite of changes in forty-seven states since 1974, in
which the states agreed to meet the requirements of the Juvenile
Justice and Delinquency Prevention Act of 1974 and reclassify
and/or divert more status offenders (Paul and Watt, 1980).

Similarly, though twenty-one states have enacted statutes to
recommend nonsecure detention for juveniles and twenty-three states
have prohibited sentencing status offenders to secure facilities (Paul
and Watt, 1980), the numbers of status offenders in short- and
long-term detention remains far too high. In 1976, 17.9 percent of the
juveniles detained in jails nationwide were awaiting hearings for
alleged status offenses (Children's Defense Fund, 1976). From 1974
to 1977, the number of status offenders in detention decreased, while
the number of status offenders incarcerated increased (Berkman and
Smith, 1980). Of those juveniles incarcerated, approximately 75
percent of the females and 20 percent of the males have been found
guilty of status offenses. In one institution for females, 90 percent of
the residents had been incarcerated for status offenses (1982). The
data also suggest that some status offenders receive longer sentences
than criminal offenders (McNeece, 1980) and that female status
offenders receive longer sentences and are incarcerated more often
than male status offenders (Grimes, 1983). McNeece (1980) also
found that in the state of Arkansas, a number of status offenders

who were placed on probation and then violated that probation were relabeled as delinquents and institutionalized.

As discussed in the section on diversion in Chapter 1, there is also evidence to suggest that diversion programs for status offenders in lieu of formal processing and institutionalization only "widen the net" and expand rather than limit state control over juveniles. Kobrin and Klein (1982) evaluated eight sites receiving federal funds to support programs to deinstitutionalize status offenders. They found a tendency to bring into these programs status offenders who would have been truly "diverted" had the programs not existed. Similarly, the Youth Service Bureau directors reported that, while the primary goal of their program was diversion, only 25 percent of their clients would have definitely been referred to juvenile court (Nejelski, 1976). It appears that the more we attempt to limit state involvement, the more extensive it becomes. We seem to have moved the agency of control from the courts to the community, but we are still detaining, processing, and penalizing juveniles for their condition or status and not their conduct (Fox, 1977).

This emphasis on condition rather than conduct is most evident in the tendency to try to "protect" females more than males. As several authors have suggested (Chesney-Lind, 1982; Huntington, 1982; Grimes, 1983), female juveniles are more likely to be arrested and adjudicated for status offenders than are male juveniles.

What can be done? There seems to be agreement that instead of diverting status offenders, we should abolish the juvenile court's jurisdiction over status offenses (Schur, 1973; Rubin, 1977). However, both status offenders and juvenile delinquents need services. Spiro (1984) conducted a survey of the careers, court treatment, and psychosocial, familial, and demographic characteristics of adjudicated "persons in need of supervision" and juvenile delinquents in Nassau County, New York. Both groups of juveniles were defined as "troubled." Their families were under stress and the functioning of the family units impaired. The status offenders were not less likely to have problems than the juvenile delinquents, though the behavior problems of the delinquents were more serious. Both showed needs for services, and the needs of both groups were left unresolved after court intervention.

What can be done? Diversion to public and private agencies has not had an impact. The use of the courts has not benefited status offenders; in fact, it may have contributed to further misbehavior among these juveniles. However, these children and their families need services. Will they receive these services if they are not "coerced" by the state? Who will pay for these services if they are not publicly funded? When the controls of the school and family do not prevent misbehaviors such as truancy and running away, what controls other than state authority will be functional? Conversely, what impact does labeling have on status offenders? Is it just to sanction a child when the child's misbehavior is only a symptom of problems in his or her family unit? What impact would a 20 percent reduction in court referrals have on the operation of the juvenile court? Could it allow for greater attention to serious juvenile crime?

The answers are not easy or readily available. However, much of the evidence suggests that the maturation process reduces contacts with the juvenile justice system (Spergel et al., 1981). Since status offenses are less serious misbehaviors, it might be best to do less when the utility of doing more is questionable. The caseload of the juvenile courts would be reduced, the possibility of stigmatization and its effect on future behavior would be removed, and the juvenile court could concentrate on serious juvenile crime.

Status offenders could be referred to public agencies specifically developed to provide services to the child and the family. The involvement of the state could not be eliminated, but its potentially punitive effect could be minimized. Currently, child protective services, foster care services, and missing and exploited child units exist. These state, county, and local agencies could be expanded to accommodate the service referral needs and periodic legal intervention needs of status offenders. Foster care services, with adequate financial and staff support, could meet the temporary shelter needs of status offenders who must be removed from their homes because of family conditions. Similarly, expanding residential treatment programs and group homes would accommodate the long-term shelter care needs. As mentioned before, some state intervention is required. If parents cannot and will not control juveniles, the state must intervene. However, processing status offenders such as juvenile delinquents is not the appropriate response. A family court that can intervene to fulfill the voids left by a malfunctioning or inadequate family unit would be more useful. Simultaneously, recognizing that our sociocultural ideal of childhood and the child is naive and unrealistic in today's society and recognizing the needs children have for status, freedom of choice, and individual rights would minimize some of the needs that juveniles seek to fulfill through misbehavior.

5

SANCTIONING DELINQUENTS

It is clear that the juvenile court was based upon the premise of "saving the child." The next stage in the juvenile justice system, corrections, is thus faced with the enormous task of rehabilitating the delinquent and providing some form of treatment on behalf of the client while simultaneously protecting the public. This chapter outlines the subcomponents of the juvenile justice correctional system: probation, institutionalization and parole, and community-based programs. The crucial issue in this chapter is concerned with the changing view of delinquency and the movement toward stricter sanctions for violent juvenile offenders.

JUVENILE PROBATION

The driving force behind the development of community-based corrections for juveniles has been the recognition that institution-alization should be used only as a last resort. As in the adult system, probation is the heart of the community corrections system, and it is a sanction that is frequently used by the court. For example, in 1979, the Bureau of Justice Statistics (1983: 75) estimated that 381,194 juveniles were under community supervision (probation and parole), compared to the 71,792 juveniles who were confined.

As defined by the President's Commission on Law Enforcement and the Administration of Justice (1967: 130), juvenile probation permits a child to remain in the community under the supervision and guidance of a probation officer as a legal status from the juvenile court. It usually involves

(1) a judicial finding that the behavior of the child has been such as to bring him or her within the purview of the court.
(2) the imposition of conditions upon his continued freedom.
(3) the provision of means of helping him meet those conditions and for determining the degree to which he needs them.

The Task Force on Juvenile Justice and Delinquency Prevention (1976: 673-674) recommends that community supervision emphasize practices consistent with the philosophy of employing the "least coercive dispositional alternative" in juvenile cases. Accordingly, the probation officer should give the juvenile full opportunity in the preparation of a treatment plan and act in accordance with the directives of the family court. Similarly, Streib (1978: 80) has strongly recommended that the role of the juvenile probation officer "should be more restrictively designed, with active supervision of all activities and written justification for all decisions." In sum, the thrust of juvenile probation is consistent with the doctrine parens patriae, emphasizing treatment and helping the youth adjust to the community.

John Augustus, the Boston shoemaker, is credited as the founder of probation for both adults and juveniles. In 1841, some fifty years before the establishment of the first juvenile court, Augustus began to speak for and assist offenders. His "caseload" included men, women, and girls. By 1863, the Children's Aid Society of Boston was extremely active in the area of probation. Here, Rufus R. Cook and Miss L. P. Burnham were concerned with providing investigations of and supervision for boys placed on probation by the police and superior courts. The official establishment of juvenile probation took place in Massachusetts in 1869. With the development of the juvenile court (see Chapter 3), juvenile probation followed the basic idea that the provision of guidance, supervision, resources, and counseling for nondangerous, low-risk juveniles would benefit the youth, his or her family, and the community (Coffey, 1974: 108).

PURPOSES OF JUVENILE PROBATION

In terms of its underlying rationales, juvenile probation is similar to its adult counterpart. The first notion is that probation offers a type of leniency. The offender is given a second chance because he or she is considered to be a good risk. Although the youth will undergo some measure of surveillance, he or she is also able to avoid the perils of incarceration and the potential problems that the stigma of a prison sentence can cause. Second, probation does involve a certain measure of policing to make certain that the youth abides by the conditions of probation. The conditions are typically designed to prevent future delinquent acts by the youth and are directly related to the offense at hand. In fact, the Commission on Accreditation for Corrections of the American Correctional Association (1978: 32-33) has recommended that conditions of probation, since they can be treated as the basis for revocation and the imposition of sentence, must be given to the youth in writing and that their receipt and their ultimate meaning should be acknowledged by the parents of the youth. Finally, probation can be considered as a form of treatment in which the probation officer either directly (the casework model) or indirectly, through referral to the appropriate agency or professional (the brokerage model), provides therapy or counseling on behalf of the youth.

TASKS OF JUVENILE PROBATION

In addition, juvenile probation should be viewed as a process in which a case is handled in different ways at different levels. The first stage is the intake process, conducted by the probation officer, to determine the cases which contain facts that would merit a formal court hearing and separate them from the cases that should be referred to other agencies for treatment and handling. Here, it is vital that the officer is familiar with the jurisdictional authority of the court and the community services available for youths.

The second and most demanding function performed by the officer is the social investigation of the history of the youth. This function is tied to the referral of the case to the juvenile court for a formal hearing. The subsequent report is extremely important, since it will serve as the basis for adjudication as well as treatment. In addition to interviewing the youth and his or her family, the investigation usually involves contact with school officials, employers, peers, and other relevant sources of information. Typically, some form of diagnostic study of the youth is also included. This information will serve as the basis for the presentence investigation. Here, the officer is faced with the difficult problem of attempting to predict the future behavior of the youth and offer recommendations to the court as to which disposition (probation or incarceration) would be most appropriate in this case and whether the release of the youth would constitute a threat to the community.

If the client is placed on probation, the final function of the probation officer is supervision. Ideally, supervision involves following a plan of treatment that has been deemed appropriate in this case. Here, the casework approach is followed. In fact, supervision clearly has a surveillance function involving a monitoring of the behavior of the youth to ensure compliance with the conditions of probation that have been established by the court. Both approaches are concerned with maintaining some contact with the client, but for different purposes. In practice, these roles are difficult for the probation officer to separate (see Marshall and Vito, 1982). In addition, there is some evidence that the individual's view of the job may affect the manner in which cases are handled. In their survey of 255 juvenile probation officers, Anderson and Spanier (1980: 510) discovered that the respondents who perceived that their major role responsibility was to provide treatment and service were significantly less likely to label juvenile acts as delinquent than those officers who felt that they should be recommending legal dispositions. This role conflict is just one of the many pressures that juvenile probation officers face.

EFFECTIVENESS OF JUVENILE PROBATION

Naturally, concerned observers of juvenile probation are most interested in the recidivism rate or the effectiveness of this sanction.

The evaluation of the effectiveness of juvenile programs will be discussed in Chapter 6. Of course, there have been numerous studies of the effectiveness of specialized juvenile probation programs (see Jones and Kravitz, 1980). Yet, in terms of "straight" probation, the key issue is whether the juvenile probationers perform better than their counterparts who have been institutionalized.

A study by Scarpitti and Stephenson (1968) attempted to answer this question by comparing the recidivism rates of 1210 adjudicated male delinquents, aged between sixteen and eighteen, from Essex County (Newark), New Jersey. Of this group, 943 youths were on probation, 100 were placed in a nonresidential guided group interaction center, 67 resided in such centers, and 100 were sent to the state reformatory. It was discovered that the probationers had the lowest (15 percent) and the reformatory boys had the highest (55 percent) recidivism rates, while both groups of residential center boys fell somewhere in between (48 and 41 percent). This general pattern remained even when only the "in-program failures" (boys who were eliminated from each type of program) were compared. As expected, it was also apparent that the boys assigned to probation were "better or easier" cases and that the best risks were assigned to probation. It is difficult to reach any sweeping conclusions based upon one study, but it is safe and accurate to say that juvenile probation attempts to limit penetration into the system and to save institutionalization as a last resort for the most serious cases.

INSTITUTIONALIZATION

In the light of the American desire to save delinquents, it is especially ironic that one of the first prisons in the world was designed to incarcerate juveniles. The Hospice at San Michele in Rome was erected by Pope Clement XI in 1704 and was designed for the treatment of wayward youth. The guiding philosophy of this institution was expiation—the atonement of sins through suffering. Two sets of clients were housed in the institution: youths under twenty years of age sentenced by the court for the commission of crimes and "incorrigible" boys who could not be controlled by their parents. The regimen followed by these boys consisted of the following (Barnes and Teeters, 1959: 334):

> The young offenders worked in association in a central hall at tasks in spinning and weaving. Chained by one foot and under a strict rule of silence, they listened to the brothers of a religious order while they droned through the Scripture of religious tracts. The incorrigible boys were kept separated, day and night, in little cubicles or cells. Large signs, hung throughout the institution, admonished "Silence." Floggings were resorted to as penalties for "past mistakes" as well as for the infraction of rules.

In this country, child-care institutions followed the development of adult prisons. Between 1824 and 1840, houses of refuge opened in New York, Boston, Philadelphia, Chicago, Cincinnati, Bangor (Maine), Richmond (Virginia), and Mobile (Alabama). According to Rothman (1971), these institutions were founded upon the basic premise that "a good dose of institutionalization" could only serve to benefit the juvenile offender, the wandering street arab, the willfully disobedient child, and the orphan to "shield them from the temptations of a sinful world." The program often followed the promise of the founders of the Philadelphia House of Refuge not to return delinquents to society until they had been exposed to "a course of rigid but not cruel or ignominious discipline" including "unrelenting supervision, mild but certain punishments for any infraction of the rules, and habits of quiet and good order at all times" (Rothman, 1971: 215). In short, the institution was to take the place of, and repair the damage caused by the failures of, the family and the community.

In the next phase of juvenile institutional development, the training (or reform) school was established. Early forms of this institution included the Lyman (Massachusetts) School for Boys (1846) and the Maine Boys Training Center (1853). In his critique of the Progressive era, Rothman (1980) writes that the training school was designed to be the modern replacement for the punitive reformatory. Reformatories, like the Elmira (New York) reformatory, were designed for young (sixteen to thirty years of age) male first offenders. Established in the 1870s, the reformatory was the centerpiece of the rehabilitation model, and it featured such new ideas as the indeterminate sentence and parole.

However, the training school was constructed along a cottage, rather than a cell-block, design, more conducive to community living and offered educational and vocational training to its charges while avoiding the hazards of corporal punishment and institutionalization. Rothman states that this institution failed to live up to its promise and fell victim to the correctional ideological battle between "conscience (rehabilitation) and convenience (custody and security)."

As Bartollas and Sieverdes (1982: 22) indicate, the emphasis in this century has been upon the implementation of a treatment regimen including both psychological treatment and specialized vocational training. In addition, the structure of juvenile institutions expanded to include such diverse entities as ranches, forestry camps, farms, reception and diagnostic centers, educational and vocational training schools, and maximum security training schools. The data in Tables 5.1 and 5.2 present information on committed delinquents in public juvenile custody facilities in 1982. In Table 5.1, we see that most incarcerated juveniles (54.2 percent) have committed a property offense, followed by violent crimes (28.4 percent). In each case, the rate for males far exceeds that of female committed delinquents. From the data in Table 5.2, the typical long-term juvenile custody resident can be viewed as male, 15.7 years old, white (but 39.3 percent of the population was black), and held in an institution. During the past decade, however, juvenile institutions have come under attack.

Criticisms of juvenile facilities have coalesced around the negative effects of incarceration. For example, Culbertson (1975) measured the effect of institutionalization upon the self-concept of boys incarcerated at the Indiana Boys School. He discovered that incarceration had a negative effect upon self-concept, especially among the boys who had never been in prison before. Such an effect could be fostered by the existence of an inmate subculture. Bartollas et al. (1976) studied the exploitation of inmates at a maximum security juvenile reformatory for boys. They classified 90 percent of the inmates as either "exploiters" or victims. The exploiters were mostly streetwise blacks who victimized other inmates for food, cigarettes, clothes, soap, and sex. There is some evidence that the

TABLE 5.1
Offenses of Committed Delinquents in
Public Juvenile Custody Facilities, 1982

Offense	Male	Female	Total
Violent crime	8,754	753	9,507
Property crime	16,616	1,496	18,112
Alcohol-related	356	73	429
Drug-related	980	141	1,121
Public order	1,467	380	1,847
Not available	2,042	372	2,418
Totals	30,215	3,219	33,434

SOURCE: Office of Juvenile Justice and Delinquency Prevention, 1983.

inmate subculture of an institution is influenced by both personal and institutional attributes. Poole and Regoli (1983) examined the factors that influenced rates of violence in four juvenile institutions. They reported that boys who engaged in violent behavior prior to their incarceration were most likely to practice institutional aggression. They also determined that when juvenile institutions concentrate their efforts upon custody and control, they may indirectly sponsor inmate violence by allowing the "pain of imprisonment" to flourish. There is little doubt that the original "child savers" did not foresee the possibility of sponsoring such damaging values in juvenile institutions. This is not the type of "community" that they sought to develop.

The crucial question here is whether juveniles have a constitutional right to treatment. The most significant case in this regard was *Nelson v. Hayne* in which the federal court upheld a categorical right to treatment under the due process clause of the Fourteenth Amendment, as well as the right to be free from cruel and unusual punishment as determined by the Eighth Amendment. In this case, plaintiffs asked for a temporary restraining order to be free from the use of corporal punishment and the use of tranquilizing drugs at Indian Boys School. In deciding in favor of the plaintiffs, the court held that a parens patriae justification for institutionalization could be upheld only if treatment is available (Senna and Siegel, 1976: 478):

In our view the "right to treatment" includes the right to minimum acceptable standards of care and treatment for juveniles and the right

TABLE 5.2
Characteristics of Long-Term Juvenile Custody Residents
in 1982

Characteristic	1982
Sex	
Male	29,762
Female	3,736
Average age in years	
Male	15.7
Female	15.3
Race	
White	19,333
Black	13,172
Other	704
Not reported	289
Reason held	
Delinquency	
Institutional	23,766
Open	7,622
Status offense:	
Institutional	615
Open	790

SOURCE: Office of Juvenile Justice and Delinquency Prevention, 1983.

to *individualized* care and treatment. Because children differ in their need for rehabilitation, individual need for treatment will differ. When a state assumes the place of a juvenile's parents, it assumes as well the parental duties, and its treatment of its juveniles should, so far as can be reasonably required, be what proper parental care would provide. Without a program of individual treatment the result may be that the juvenile will not be rehabilitated, but warehoused, and that at the termination of detention they will likely be incapable of taking their proper places in free society, their interests and those of the state and the school thereby being defeated.

Although the U.S. Supreme Court has not declared that juveniles have such a right, the *Nelson* case is significant because it is the first federal court decision to affirm a constitutional right to treatment (Senna and Siegel, 1976: 422). Of course, such findings spurred the development of a decarceration movement that attempted to restrict the use of incarceration for juveniles.

DECARCERATION

The greatest proponent of decarceration is Jerome Miller. After his appointment as youth commissioner for the state of Massachusetts in 1969, Miller closed the major juvenile institutions in the state and utilized small group homes and other existing community-based correctional facilities and services to handle delinquents. A major study of the effects of decarceration in Massachusetts was conducted by Coates et al. (1978: 149-154), in which the recidivism rates of a sample of boys released from the traditional institutions in 1968 were compared to a sample of boys placed under community supervision in 1974. Coates et al. discovered that the rates of recidivism for both a reappearance in court (74 versus 66 percent) and for either probation or commitment (55 versus 47 percent) were slightly higher for the boys under decarceration. The same pattern was discovered for girls (reappearance was 37 versus 24 percent and probation/commitment was 25 versus 10 percent) One of the key reasons for these negative findings cited by the authors was that the decarceration movement had failed to plug into community networks (Coates et al., 1978: 173):

> Instead of having "institution kids" we now have a new group of "agency kids." They are generally treated better, but their experience in these agencies is still quite foreign to the worlds in which they live. If these private agencies are to prevent recidivism better than the training school model, they must take the risk of becoming involved in the community to a more significant degree than simply retaining a "community board."

Thus, community involvement is still the key to successful integration of delinquents. Institutionalization can cause new problems without treating the original ones, and transfer to the community without true involvement can fail to combat delinquency effectively.

However, there is some doubt that states other than Massachusetts ever fully committed themselves to decarceration of juveniles. In Table 5.3, we can see that between 1979 and 1982, twenty-three states experienced an increase in both the number and the rate of juveniles incarcerated in public juvenile custody systems. Overall, the total number of juveniles incarcerated increased by 5.4 percent, and the rate of juveniles incarcerated per 100,000 population went up by 10.2 percent, between 1979 and 1982. Reuterman and Hughes (1984) examined data taken from a sample of juvenile detention facilities in the late 1960s and again in the late 1970s to determine whether juvenile justice recommendations concerning reduced use of incarceration (belief in the use of the "least restrictive environment") were being followed. They discovered that the average number of yearly admissions per 1000 population served and the percentage of facilities exceeding a recommended level of 20 percent had increased. In addition, a survey of juvenile institutional staff indicated that they believed that secure custody (first) and rehabilitation (second) were the major responsibilities of detention facilities. This evidence leads to the conclusion that decarceration may have been a widely held, but not a widely practiced, philosophy for juveniles.

PAROLE

As with adults, parole for juveniles involves the early release from incarceration of an inmate by the parole board. Typically, the release is subject to certain conditions which, if violated by the parolee, can result in parole revocation and return to the institution. With juveniles, parole is viewed as an aftercare procedure with release to the community, specifically designed to facilitate readjustment. Here, the conflicting purpose is the protection of the community. As with probation, the casework versus surveillance dichotomy appears.

Edelfonso and Hartinger (1976: 207-208) report that, in the early nineteenth century, minors released from houses of refuge in Pennsylvania and New York were indentured to local families. The family then assumed total responsibility for the care of the minor and decided when the juvenile had earned his or her freedom. The modern

TABLE 5.3
Characteristics of Public Juvenile Custody Systems
in the United States, 1982

State	Number	Percentage Change Since 1979	Number per 100,000 Age Eligible Population	Percentage Change Since 1979
Alabama	712	+8.0	133	+1.2
Alaska	170	+3.0	283	+16.9
Arizona	587	−10.7	160	−10.6
Arkansas	290	−20.0	95	−13.6
California	13,449	+14.9	456	+20.6
Colorado	543	−11.1	145	−9.9
Connecticut	130	−30.1	46	−22.0
Delaware	240	−1.6	316	+7.5
D.C.	338	−30.6	497	−26.5
Florida	2,199	−4.2	189	−4.1
Georgia	1,319	+2.0	198	+4.2
Hawaii	135	+0.7	110	−0.9
Idaho	185	+5.7	136	−0.7
Illinois	1,689	+25.9	134	+34.0
Indiana	1,182	+2.5	163	+9.4
Iowa	360	−9.3	98	−3.0
Kansas	600	−1.6	207	+1.5
Kentucky	614	−17.0	126	−13.1
Louisiana	1,396	+35.4	263	+37.7
Maine	220	+22.9	147	+30.1
Maryland	1,103	+9.5	202	+20.9
Massachusetts	143	+4.0	24	+9.0
Michigan	1,760	−6.5	165	+1.9
Minnesota	655	−18.8	124	−12.7
Mississippi	459	+15.3	124	+18.1
Missouri	906	−10.7	171	−5.5
Montana	154	−11.0	148	−8.6
Nebraska	233	−0.4	117	+2.6
Nevada	499	+7.7	420	+4.7
New Hampshire	130	−23.5	106	−20.3
New Jersey	1,747	+16.4	186	+26.5
New Mexico	423	+4.0	321	+4.7
New York	1,521	+10.0	96	+20.0
North Carolina	754	−8.0	131	−6.4
North Dakota	93	−7.9	108	−6.9
Ohio	3,082	+7.9	220	+9.4
Oklahoma	519	−12.9	131	−10.3
Oregon	857	+1.9	265	+6.0
Pennsylvania	1,178	−0.8	81	+6.6
Rhode Island	94	+10.6	81	+19.1
South Carolina	803	+4.8	213	+7.6

TABLE 5.3 Continued

State	Number	Percentage Change Since 1979	Number per 100,000 Age Eligible Population	Percentage Change Since 1979
South Dakota	169	+19.9	190	+26.7
Tennessee	1,055	−14.5	176	−11.1
Texas	1,980	+21.1	111	+15.6
Utah	161	−42.1	70	−48.5
Vermont	0	0.0	0	0.0
Virginia	1,520	+3.2	221	+8.9
Washington	1,240	+24.5	239	+22.6
West Virginia	124	−58.9	48	−58.6
Wisconsin	559	−20.3	90	−14.3
Wyoming	173	−1.2	237	−2.9
Totals	50,399	+5.4	184	+10.2

SOURCE: Adapted from Office of Juvenile Justice and Delinquency Prevention, 1983.

system is more comparable to the methods used with adult inmates. However, several experts agree that juvenile parolees are not offered the same level of service as their adult counterparts or their juvenile peers on probation (Bartollas and Miller, 1978: 81; Edelfonso and Hartinger, 1976: 208).

Once the juvenile is incarcerated, the parole release decision determines the length of incarceration for that person. One study by Hussey (1976) examined the factors that influenced this crucial, discretionary decision for 424 juvenile males who were released from one institution in one year. He determined that the factors associated with release differed across racial groups. For whites, the release was predicated upon factors "congruent with the juvenile justice philosophy," such as the amount of parental education, evidence of psychological disorder, socioeconomic class, and the degree to which the family used welfare resources. Among blacks and Mexican Americans, variables of a more criminal nature, such as prior escapes, criminal history of the father, severity of the offense, and age at first delinquent commitment, were closely associated with the probability of release. On the basis of this evidence, Hussey concluded that "the race of the delinquent provides the primary basis for subsequent consideration of the decision to parole." It is difficult to draw far-reaching conclusions on the basis of one study, but the forces affecting parole release must be considered.

PROBATION AND PAROLE REVOCATION: LEGAL RESTRICTIONS

The common link between probation and parole is that each affords the juvenile some conditional liberty from institutionalization. Therefore, the revocation of probation or parole release involves a basic threat and loss of freedom for the juvenile. As in other areas of the law, the rights enjoyed by adults under the probation and/or parole system have been extended to juveniles. Basically, the loss of liberty that a revocation represents has been determined to be significant enough to entitle the probationer or the parolee to due process of law as required by the Fourteenth Amendment (see *Morrissey v. Brewer, Gagnon v. Scarpelli;* del Carmen, 1985). In parole revocation proceedings, the courts have ruled that juveniles are entitled to adult due process safeguards such as the right to a hearing and the right to be represented by counsel at such proceedings (Davis, 1980: 6-35).

Specifically, with regard to probation, the courts have held that juveniles are entitled to the same procedural due process rights as adults, including written notice, disclosure of evidence showing a violation, the opportunity to be heard and to present evidence, the right to confrontation and cross-examination, an impartial examiner, and a statement of the reasons that probation was revoked. The right to counsel in such proceedings has been generally upheld on a case-by-case basis (Davis, 1980: 6-36). Overall, the courts have ruled that the conditions of probation should not be unusually broad and should have some demonstrable relationship to the protection of the individual and the community (Senna and Siegel, 1976: 401-408).

EFFECTIVENESS OF JUVENILE PAROLE

Data on recidivism rates for juvenile parolees on a nationwide basis are difficult to come by. For example, the American Correctional Association (1984: 43) reported that, as of July 1, 1983, the range of juvenile offender recidivism rates varied from 3 percent in Wyoming to 52.4 percent in Colorado. However, recidivism was defined in different ways across the jurisdictions (see Chapter 6), and twenty states failed to report. For this reason, it is often necessary to examine individual studies of juvenile parole (aftercare) to get some accurate grasp of the extent of recidivism.

One of the most extensive evaluations of the effectiveness of juvenile parole supervision was the California Community Treatment Project. This project attempted to ascertain the effect of intensive supervision on juveniles. Juvenile parolees were screened on the basis of their Interpersonal Maturity Level (I-level) and then assigned at random to a specialized (twelve juveniles per officer) or regular caseload. Palmer (1971: 84-86) reported that males served by the project had lower revocation and recommitment rates (42 versus 64 percent), lower unfavorable discharge rates from parole supervision (8 versus 22 percent), and similar rates of rearrest (82 versus 81 percent). Among females, an almost identical pattern was evident, with the experimental-group girls demonstrating a lower rate of revocation or recommitment (34 versus 48 percent) a lower rate of unfavorable discharge (0 versus 17 percent), but a higher rate of rearrest (27 versus 0 percent), in comparison with the control-group girls. However, Palmer's findings were extensively reanalyzed by both Lerman (1975) and Martinson (1974, 1976). Lerman determined that the difference in revocation rates between the two groups was largely due to changes in reporting practices by parole officers participating in the experiment. Literally, the experimental parole officers were less likely to revoke their clients even when those clients had committed an offense against persons or property (Lerman, 1975: 60). Martinson (1976) wrote that the CTP evaluation had failed to identify exactly what part of the treatment was responsible for the favorable outcomes.

The CTP experiment and the controversy surrounding its findings indicates the difficulty in ascertaining the effectiveness of juvenile parole supervision. Questions surrounding the evaluation of juvenile programs will be discussed in more detail in Chapter 6.

CRITICAL ISSUE:
THE DANGEROUS JUVENILE OFFENDER

Recent issues have come together to begin a movement against the serious, violent juvenile offender. This movement calls for a fundamental refocusing of the sanctioning capacities of the juvenile justice system. As in the adult correctional system, the ideal of rehabilitation has been called into question, and it has been determined that juvenile corrections should stress deterrence and incapacitation in the future.

This trend is based upon findings of current research concerning the extent and nature of juvenile crime. The underlying conclusion is that a small percentage of juveniles are responsible for the bulk of serious crime committed in the United States. For example, in their pioneering study of a 1945 Philadelphia birth cohort, Wolfgang et al. (1972) reported that a minority of the youth were "chronic recidivists" (6 percent of the entire cohort of 3475) and that they were responsible for a total of 5305 offenses. The chronic delinquents committed 63 percent of the Uniform Crime Reports Index Offenses of the cohort, including 71 percent of the homicides, 73 percent of the rapes, 82 percent of the robberies, and 69 percent of the aggravated assaults. In a follow-up study of a 1958 Philadelphia birth cohort, Tracy and Figlio (1982) reported an even higher rate of serious crime for the chronic delinquent group. In this study, the chronic offenders constituted only 15 percent of the total sample, but they were responsible for 82 percent of all Index Crime arrests. Again, this small group of juvenile offenders was responsible for 61 percent of the homicides, 76 percent of the rapes, 73 percent of the robberies, and 65 percent of the aggravated assaults. Similarly, a study of a 1956-1960 Columbus, Ohio, birth cohort by Hamparian et al. (1978) revealed that only 2 percent of the cohort had committed a violent offense. Overall, these findings have sponsored a "get tough" movement against the serious juvenile offender.

This movement is evident in the recommendations of two national committees. The National Advisory Commission for Juvenile Justice and Delinquency Prevention (1984) has recommended that the federal government should change its posture toward juveniles (as evidenced by the 1974 Juvenile Justice Act) and "focus primarily on the serious, violent, or chronic offender." Attacking the premises of labeling theory and decarceration, the commission (1984: 7) stated that the previously held conclusion that the juvenile justice system was responsible for delinquency was erroneous:

> Unsubstantiated theory governed policy: minimize punishment of juveniles whenever possible, rely only on prevention rather than emphasize correction and deterrence to reduce delinquency. . . . Ten years of experience and current evaluations persuade us that this medicine has not produced a cure.

Similarly, the National Council of Juvenile and Family Court Judges (1984) has issued thirty-eight specific recommendations concerning the serious juvenile offender; among these recommendations, the council calls for guidelines to reduce sentencing disparities for serious, chronic, or violent offenders, fitting the severity of the disposition to the severity of the present and past offenses, and the establishment of secure facilities for high-risk juveniles, along with substance abuse programs and mental treatment facilities for juveniles (see also Mathias, 1984).

Evidence to support such a movement is somewhat mixed. Murray and Cox (1979) conducted an exhaustive study of chronic juvenile delinquents who were treated in different ways in Illinois. Their analysis of 317 chronic, inner-city juvenile offenders from Chicago revealed that, before their institutional commitment, each juvenile had been arrested at least thirteen times, with at least eight of these arrests for serious Index Crimes. A comparison was made between the outcomes generated by this group and a sample of 266 youths who had been placed in community-based programs (at-home services, community-based residential services, wilderness programs, out-of-town residential camps, and "intensive care" residential therapeutic programs) operated by Unified Delinquency Intervention Services (UDIS). The authors reported that the UDIS placements were not as effective as institutionalization in the reduction of postrelease arrest rates. A final comparison was added so that the effectiveness of probation supervision could be ascertained. The final analysis revealed that crimes among chronic offenders may have been reduced from 50 to 70 percent, depending upon the type of intervention used. In other words, the research conducted by Murray and Cox demonstrates that custodial treatment of chronic offenders may have a beneficial effect in reducing recidivism.

However, an evaluation of a new "just deserts" system of sentencing guidelines established in the state of Washington did not yield positive results. Schneider (1984) studied a sample of 2400 juvenile offenders drawn before and after the sentencing change. Under the postreform system, violent juvenile offenders experienced a definite increase in the probability of commitment: 92 percent of the postreform sentences for this group reflected institutionalization. Yet there was no discernible effect upon the recidivism rates of juvenile offenders following the sentencing reform. Schneider indicates that the absence of a recidivism effect may have been due to changes in law enforcement policies concerning the contact and arrest of juveniles. The police may have been less likely to refer juveniles under the new system.

There is little doubt that the "get tough" movement is just beginning. Cracking down on serious juvenile offenders may very well be the next revolution in juvenile justice.

CONCLUSION

It is clear that policy in juvenile corrections has undergone a number of changes and fluctuations throughout history. The rehabilitation model is under severe attack, and punishment of the serious juvenile offender has been established as a priority. However, old ideals die hard. As a survey by Cullen et al. (1983) indicates, many individuals still believe in "child saving." A sample of the general public, prison guards, legislators, judges, lawyers, correctional administrators, and prison inmates expressed the strongest overall support (81.6 percent of the sample) for the statement, "It would be irresponsible for us to stop trying to rehabilitate juvenile delinquents and thus save them from a life of crime." The desire for punishment may still not outstrip the parens patriae philosophy of juvenile corrections.

6

DETERMINING PROGRAM
SUCCESS OR FAILURE

As we have witnessed, the problem of delinquency has spawned numerous attempts to combat its rise and spread. All segments of the juvenile justice system have developed specialized programs to apprehend, treat, sanction, or otherwise handle juvenile offenders. To many persons involved in the field, the "bottom line" of these attempts has basically been, "Is the program able to reduce delinquency and prevent recidivism?" In this chapter, we will consider the process of determining program success or failure, the basic issues surrounding the conduct of evaluation research, and the manner in which program effectiveness can be addressed. Special attention will be given to one well-publicized attempt to reduce delinquency, the "Scared Straight!" program.

THE NATURE AND PURPOSE
OF EVALUATION RESEARCH

As defined by Rossi and Wright (1977: 5), evaluation research is "any scientifically based activity undertaken to assess the operation and impact of public policies and the action programs introduced to implement these policies." The central purpose of evaluation research is the assessment of the extent to which a social program achieves its goals. It is also necessary to make the determination that success was actually a function of program activity. The evaluation of programs designed to reduce delinquency, for example, would basically include the four steps identified by Suchman (1967: 28):

(1) formulation of the program's objectives
(2) identification of the proper criteria to be used in measuring success
(3) determination and explanation of the degree of success
(4) recommendations for future program activity

Evaluation research should also be concerned with the effect of the program upon the group (such as adjudicated delinquents) that the program is designed to serve. Typically, research designs are utilized to assess the extent to which goals and objectives are realized and to identify the factors associated with success and failure. Ideally, the results of evaluation research not only should address the attainment of goals and objectives but also should provide information and feedback and indicate future directions for the program (reduction, alteration, continuation, or abolition).

In their review of the impact of juvenile diversion programs, Gibbons and Blake (1976: 412) identified three basic types of program evaluation:

(1) The *effectiveness evaluation* is concerned with whether the program was directed, in fact, at the target population for which it was intended, the ease with which the program obtained access to target clients, and the obstacles to the inauguration of the program with the appropriate clients.
(2) The *efficiency (process) evaluation* studies the frequency and quality of service delivery and deals with the extent to which the processes, activities, and stratagems of interventions were actually implemented.
(3) The *impact (outcome) evaluation* focuses on the achievement of the intended ends or consequences of intervention and typically includes a consideration of the recidivism rate of the program participants.

In addition, there may be some consideration of the impact of the program on the juvenile justice system. For example, an evaluation of a diversion program could consider whether the program had some impact upon the rate of referrals to the juvenile court. Of course, it is possible and even desirable to pursue all three types of evaluation simultaneously. If the program does not serve its clients in an effective and efficient fashion, there is little reason to believe that the program will produce a desirable outcome. Unfortunately, evaluation research is plagued by a number of constraints that directly impinge upon the ability of the information to serve as a basis for policymaking.

ESTABLISHING PROGRAM GOALS: DEFINING THE CRITERIA FOR SUCCESS

One of the major difficulties in evaluation research is the translation of the goals of the project into measurable indicators of achievement. The goals should be directly related to the mission of the program and should generally reflect the scope of its operations. However, because of the political nature of programs, it is not uncommon to see such ambiguous and far-reaching goals as "reducing recidivism" or "preventing delinquency." As Weiss (1975: 13-26) has indicated, social action programs (such as delinquency preventive programs) are basically "political creatures" that have often emerged from political bargaining. The reputations of program sponsors (such as politicians or legislators), the careers of program administrators, the jobs of staff members, and the expectations of the clientele are dependent upon the overall assessment of program results. Hazy or exceedingly broad goals may be politically acceptable for the simple reason that they are so ambiguous that a final determination regarding success or failure may be very difficult to make. Also, very broad goals are capable of generating a great deal of public support.

In addition, Glaser (1973: 4-6) has identified another reason for "goal displacement"—the fact that several levels of program goals often exist. Glaser identifies the existence of two levels of goals: manifest and latent. Manifest, or "official," goals are proclaimed in the legislation, directives, or formal announcements under which programs are created. It is here that global goals, such as "reducing delinquency," are often born. On the other hand, latent goals are those that reflect the actual day-to-day practices and procedures within the program. For example, the manifest goal of a juvenile halfway house may be to "reduce delinquency," but its programs may be based upon providing treatment for juveniles with a drug problem. Curing drug abuse would be an example of a latent goal. Here, the research should first focus upon whether the program participants are served by the program, abstain from drug abuse, and then make a determination regarding recidivism. We would not expect a program client who was not served by the program and then returned to drugs to refrain from delinquency behavior (see Vito, 1982).

In terms of the evaluation, the goals of the program should reflect its true operations. It is possible and desirable to carry out the evaluation on a number of levels and thus to consider both manifest and latent goals. However, another problem looms in terms of the assessment of program success and failure: the feasibility of accurately measuring program goals.

THE PROBLEMS WITH RECIDIVISM RATES

Delinquency prevention programs have a long and somewhat undistinguished history of performance. Typically, these programs have generated research designs of such poor quality that conclusions regarding the overall effectiveness of delinquency prevention cannot be assessed. For example, Wright and Dixon (1978) reviewed 6600 abstracts of delinquency prevention reports published during the period from 1964 to 1974 and determined that only 96 reports contained some empirical data on program effectiveness. Similarly, Lundman et al. (1976) examined more than 1000 citations of delinquency prevention programs and discovered only 25 that had some indication of program performance. Naturally, until accurate research is conducted, broad conclusions cannot be made.

The inability of programs to conduct accurate research may be due to many factors, including lack of funds, time pressures, inadequately trained staff, and poor research methodology (see Adams, 1975). Yet one of the most basic problems has its roots in the nature of recidivism as an outcome measure.

Recidivism is the outcome variable that is most often used to evaluate the effectiveness of delinquency prevention programs. It is a "commonsense" measure in that persons in general assume that they understand its meaning. If a juvenile has recidivated, he or she has returned to delinquency. Yet, as Wilkins (1969: 44) has written, this basic definition requires close consideration.

What has been done to offenders, and particularly to those offenders variously labeled recidivists, has been assumed to be the direct outcome of their actions, in a simple cause-effect relationship. This has enabled the acceptance of the false logic that the behavior of the recidivist provides sufficient definitions and that it has not been necessary to look any further into the defining process.

Here, the crucial question is, "How is recidivism measured?" Typically, recidivism is defined as a new arrest, conviction, or incarceration over a specified time period. In addition, it is possible for a juvenile to be considered a recidivist not for committing a new crime, but for failure to maintain the conditions of probation or parole—a "technical violation" (Wilkins, 1969: 13). A juvenile can also become a recidivist by committing a crime that would not be considered a crime if it were committed by an adult—a "status offense." The choice made by the researcher to define the manner in which recidivism will be measured thus has a definite effect upon the findings of the research. For example, in their sample of 1806 adult federal prisoners serving a maximum term of more than a year and a day, Hoffman and Stone-Meierhoffer (1980) found that during the first year of release, 29 percent of the prisoners had been arrested, 15.4 percent had been convicted, 12.6 percent had been sentenced to sixty days or more, and 8.7 percent had been sentenced to prison. Within this sample, there are four different recidivism rates, each of which conveys different information.

To make matters worse, not all recidivists are arrested, let alone convicted or incarcerated. Reliance upon official records does not produce a recidivism rate that includes all persons who have committed a new offense. There is also the possibility that official records are biased in that they reflect the behaviors of officials within the system. For example, Chambliss (1984) has reported that the police and even school officials either looked the other way or did not even consider the possibility that the "Saints" (a group of upper- and middle-class boys) were committing delinquent acts, while the "Roughnecks" (a group of lower-class boys) were routinely suspected and sanctioned. Chambliss writes that the Saints often committed more serious offenses (such as drunken driving) than the Roughnecks, but the Roughnecks were more likely to get a record, because their offenses were more visible and limited to a definite geographical area. For this reason, some juvenile delinquency can go "undetected." Therefore, through the use of official statistics, the research can inherit the biases contained in the enforcement practices of the juvenile justice system.

For this reason, the "self-report" technique was developed. Basically, the self-report method goes directly to the source (the juvenile) and directly asks the subject to reveal the number and type of delinquent acts committed over a certain period of time. This method of collecting data on delinquency has a long history (see Hindelang et al., 1981), and it directly questions the accuracy and validity of official statistics. The self-report method is designed to overcome any biases that may exist within the juvenile justice system (such as concentration upon poor, urban minority group males) and to uncover delinquent acts that would otherwise go unreported.

Still, there are some questions about the accuracy of data obtained via the self-report method. First of all, the research must be concerned about the welfare of the juvenile. Why should the juvenile come forward and confess if he or she will be punished as a result? Lundman and Scarpitti (1978) have stated that researchers in this area must be mindful of the consequences of the research for the juveniles. Second, how do we know that the juvenile is telling the truth and not simply boasting, bragging, or trying to foul up the research project? Nettler (1978: 108) has severely questioned the accuracy of self-report data and disagrees with other experts (see Hirschi et al., 1980) that official statistics should be replaced by these data.

Another problem with recidivism studies is the length of the follow-up period. As Pepinsky (1980: 247) has noted, the common belief is that the longer the offender stays out of trouble with the law, the less likely he or she is to get into trouble, and that recidivism should begin to be counted as soon as offenders have the opportunity to commit new offenses. Evaluation studies of delinquency prevention programs tend to have short (for example, one-year) follow-up periods because decision makers desire quick and timely information about the effectiveness of such projects. Here again, the study of Hoffman and Stone-Meierhoffer (1980: 56) demonstrated that the length of the follow-up period can have a definite impact upon the dimension of recidivism rates. After six years, 60.4 percent of their sample had been arrested, 41.7 percent had been convicted, 34.3 percent had been incarcerated for sixty days or more, and 27.5 percent had been sentenced to prison. These rates were much higher than those recorded for the same sample after a one-year period. The problem here is that the length of the follow-up period, not the project itself, has a direct effect upon recidivism rates.

The final problem with recidivism is that it is a negative measure of outcome and fails to consider any positive results. A study should also include some measure of success (Glaser, 1973: 22):

> Indeed, those who are nonrecidivist or are abstinent are also far from uniform: they differ in the extent to which they have actually ceased their prior deviant behavior or merely avoided detection, as well as in the extent to which they have achieved other people-changing goals, such as becoming economically self-sufficient and meeting their obligations to dependents.

> Including some measure of success is a vitally important form of feedback. It gives program managers some indication of where things may be going right and where their further efforts may bring the best return.

Overall, it is clear that there are some definite problems in the consideration of recidivism in evaluations of delinquency prevention programs. To consider fully the range of problems faced in evaluation research, let us examine one particular program and the wide range of attention that this type of approach to delinquency prevention has received.

CRITICAL ISSUE:
REVIEWING THE EVALUATIONS OF
SCARING JUVENILES STRAIGHT

Often, programs for juveniles are based upon commonsense assumptions and fail to refer to both past attempts and criminological theory. If these steps are taken, realistic expectations can be established. These basic premises were ignored in the establishment of the Juvenile Awareness Program at the Rahway State Prison in New Jersey (Scared Straight!). The history of the program and initial evaluation results are presented in frank detail in a text by James O. Finckenauer (1982). This text provides a close look at the evaluation process surrounding a delinquency prevention program. A brief review of the Scared Straight! program and recent research on similar programs will demonstrate the basic premises of evaluation research and provide some insight into the effectiveness of delinquency prevention programs.

There were a number of commonsense assumptions behind the Scared Straight! program. First, the program took a page from deterrence theory and exposed juveniles who were headed for trouble to the realities of prison life. The exposure would come from inmates who had been through the experience. They would share with the juveniles their experiences in the criminal justice system. Here, aversion therapy and behavior modification would also be utilized. The inmates eventually adopted a rough confrontation approach with the juveniles. The expectation was that this type of approach would literally scare the juveniles straight. Awareness of what was in store for them if they continued along their present path would steer the juveniles away from delinquency. The initial sponsors of the program were the inmates themselves, the Lifers' Group at Rahway State Prison. Apparently, they wished to make some type of contribution to society and put their long prison sentence to constructive use. In fact, this program was no different from several others that had been established in the United States. The difference in terms of public awareness was that this program became the subject of a documentary that received wide exposure and won both an Emmy and an Academy Award. The film, and its statements concerning widespread effectiveness, led to a bandwagon approach in states that did not have such programs, with a public eager for a simple solution to a complex problem (see Cavender, 1981; Homant, 1981).

Finckenauer examines Scared Straight! as a program and as a phenomenon common to delinquency prevention programs. Most programs are plagued by the "panacea phenomenon"—the search for a cure-all for the delinquency problem. In fact, Finckenauer (1982: 4-5) proposes that delinquency prevention programs often fall victim to a four-stage, cyclical process in which (1) a cure-all is proposed, (2) the "hype" surrounding the program grows and spreads dramatically, (3) frustration caused by the failure of the program crushes hopes and, perhaps, the program itself, and (4) the cycle begins anew with a different approach. This thesis suggests a way out of the quagmire by sponsoring realistic expectations about the delinquency prevention programs.

Finckenauer's study provides information that basically follows the three types of evaluation previously outlined by Gibbons and Blake (1978). First, the effectiveness evaluation is primarily concerned with whether the program reached its target population—the clients for whom the program was designed. Initially, the Lifers' Group stated that the program was established for all juveniles: the Good (no involvement in crime), the Bad (guilty of minor infractions), and the Ugly (serious involvement in crime). However, the implication was that the program would be most effective with the Ugly group, since it could be demonstrated that they were on the road to prison. In Finckenauer's (1982: 135) evaluation, it was determined that 41 percent of the juveniles who visited Rahway had no prior record of delinquency. Nevertheless, the program appeared to obtain referrals with great ease. In fact, Finckenauer (1982: 69) reports that the program expanded very rapidly. By January 1977, the number of visits to Rahway had increased from the original one visit per week to two visits per day, five days a week. Thus, the program appeared to have no difficulty in attracting clients. However, the type of client who would best benefit from this approach was not clearly defined. The idea that the program was suitable for all juveniles was an early indication of the unrealistic expectations surrounding this program.

In what can be termed the process evaluation, Finckenauer documents the manner in which the program was implemented. Again, the initial sponsors of the project were the inmates themselves. It was necessary for them to obtain approval from the superintendent of the prison and then to obtain referrals from outside agencies. Judge George Nicola was approached, and he soon became a firm supporter of the program. The format of the sessions evolved over time to the point where the shock-confrontation approach, clearly demonstrated in the film, developed. The question here is, "To what extent did this program represent an effective form of therapy?" In spite of its ability clearly to demonstrate the realities of prison life, the program was little more than a field trip. There were little or no follow-up services provided to the juveniles after they returned to their homes and communities. The program was founded upon the best intentions of a group of inmates and a judge who wished to do something constructive about juvenile delinquency, but Scared Straight! was never a program in the true sense of the word. The goals and intervention strategy were not clearly specified, developed, and planned. The implementation of the program was spontaneous rather than strategically developed.

Of course, it is the impact or outcome evaluation that is considered the "bottom line." Finckenauer frankly describes his difficulties in establishing an experimental design for his research (for a full specification of the types of research designs, see Adams, 1975) and his problems in obtaining research data. His design was not perfect, and the results must be judged accordingly; however, he did attempt to consider a number of outcome measures of recidivism. First, recidivism was simply dichotomized as success or failure (any type of new involvement). Also, type of delinquency was weighted by seriousness (success = 0), by classification as a juvenile in need of supervision (JINS – status offenses = 1), or a juvenile delinquent (criminal = 2) offense. Finally, fifteen members of the experimental group were interviewed to obtain their impressions about the project and self-report information on their behavior following the visit.

Overall, the results were not encouraging. In sum, the experimental group had a higher rate of failure (41.3 versus 11.4 percent). This pattern did not change even when prior record was taken into account. Members of the experimental group with (48.2 percent) and without (31.6 percent) a prior record had a higher recidivism rate than did the members of the control group (21.4 and 4.8 percent, respectively). In terms of the seriousness of the new offense, the experimental group did significantly worse than the control group.

Finally, the results of the self-report study revealed that a number of the juveniles who officially appeared to be successful did commit some delinquent acts. Of the seventeen experimental group juveniles, fifteen were officially considered to be successful, but all of them had actually committed some type of minor offense (such as drinking, skipping school, destroying property, or smoking marijuana).

On the basis of this information, Finckenauer concluded that the experimental group was more seriously delinquent than the control group and that the program failed to reduce delinquency. As could be predicted, the outcry from supporters of the program was vociferous. Finckenauer's findings were attacked and questioned on the basis of this methodology and even his intentions and interest in conducting the study. Nevertheless, recent evaluation findings of similar programs seem to support Finckenauer's contentions about the Scared Straight! approach.

The effectiveness of the oldest juvenile awareness program in the United States, the San Quentin (California) Squires program, was evaluated by Lewis (1983). The procedures followed in the Squires program are very similar to Scared Straight!, with the crucial exception that "scare tactics" are not utilized and juveniles in the program take part in three sessions. The Lewis evaluation utilized an experimental design. Males aged between fourteen and eighteen with an average number of 7.4. previous arrests were assigned at random to experimental (N = 53) and control (N = 55) groups. The analysis revealed that there was no significant difference in arrest rates after a twelve-month follow-up (experimentals = 81.2 percent, controls =

67.3 percent). It was also determined that the older members of the experimental group were arrest-free longer than were the older controls, but they had committed more serious delinquent offenses than had the controls. Lewis (1983: 222) concluded that "seriously delinquent youth cannot be turned around by short-term programs such as Squires and Rahway" and that a "pattern for high-risk youth suggested that the Squires program may have been more detrimental to them." In short, like Scared Straight!, there was some evidence that the program was sponsoring rather than preventing delinquency.

Similarly, Buckner and Chesney-Lind (1983) reported their findings from an evaluation of Hawaii's Stay Straight program. Like the Squires program, Stay Straight does not feature scare tactics. It emphasizes the "experience of prisoners" with factual storytelling and advice rather than intimidation. Only youth with one prior arrest were referred to the program. The research design featured 300 juveniles: 100 males and 50 females in each group. The experimental and comparison groups were matched on the basis of sex, age, race, and prior record to ensure comparability. A one-year follow-up was utilized, and "simple recidivism" was defined as at least one subsequent arrest. Rearrest rates were reported as follows: experimental males, 41 percent; experimental females, 22 percent; comparison males, 37 percent; and comparison females, 32 percent—differences that were not statistically significant. However, closer examination revealed some damaging findings for the program. Females who attended sessions had a significantly higher number of subsequent arrests. Experimental males had a significantly higher number of subsequent arrests that resulted in a formal charge. Buckner and Chesney-Lind (1983: 240-245) correctly indicate that these findings may be due to factors other than the program, including the fact that referred youth may have had a "higher delinquency potential." In addition, it is important to note that, in terms of deterrence theory, prisoners can guarantee only severity, not certainty, of punishment. Yet Buckner and Chesney-Lind (1983: 245) reach the same basic conclusion as the previous authors: "It is unrealistic to expect that any single experience, no matter how profound, would have a significant and long lasting impact on a problem so complicated and intractable as juvenile delinquency."

CONCLUSION

This review of the prisoner-run delinquency prevention programs reveals that careful planning with an eye to the experience of previous programs and criminological theory is necessary to design effective programs. Good intentions can lead to dangerous, unrealistic expectations. Here, it is important to consider some of the conclusions drawn by Lundman and Scarpitti (1978) following their review of published research on delinquency prevention programs:

(1) Researchers should expect future projects to be unsuccessful.
(2) The theoretical foundations of future delinquency prevention programs should be expanded to include sociological as well as psychological understandings of the causes of delinquency.
(3) Researchers involved in future delinquency prevention projects should explore the possibility of employing additional and more sensitive indicators of delinquent behavior.

Evaluation research can play an important role in the development of delinquency prevention projects. It can provide valid information and feedback about the progress of programs and help make a determination regarding program success or failure. If valid conclusions are to be made and effective programs developed, evaluation research must play a role.

REFERENCES

ADAMS, S. (1975) Evaluation Research in Corrections: A Practical Guide. Washington, DC: National Institute of Law Enforcement and Criminal Justice.

ALSAGER v. DISTRICT COURT (1975) 406 F. Supp. 10 (S.D. Iowa).

American Correctional Association (1984) Vital Statistics in Corrections. College Park, MD: Author.

ANDERSON, E. A. and G. B. SPANIER (1980) "Treatment of delinquent youth: the influence of the juvenile probation officer's perceptions of self and youth." Criminology 17 (February): 505-514.

ARIES, P. (1962) Centuries of Childhood: A Social History of Family Life. New York: Alfred A. Knopf.

ARNOLD, W. R. (1971) "Race and ethnicity relative to other factors in juvenile court dispositions." American Journal of Sociology 67: 211-227.

BARNES, H. E. and N. K. TEETERS (1959) New Horizons in Criminology. Englewood Cliffs, NJ: Prentice-Hall.

BARTOLLAS, C. and S. J. MILLER (1978) The Juvenile Offender: Control, Correction, and Treatment. Boston: Holbrook Press.

BARTOLLAS, C. and C. M. SIEVERDES (1982) "Juvenile correctional institutions: a policy statement." Federal Probation 46, 3: 22-26.

BARTOLLAS, C., S. J. MILLER, and S. DINITZ (1976) Juvenile Victimization: The Institutional Paradox. New York: Halsted Press.

BERKMAN, D. J. and C. P. SMITH (1980) Status Offenses and the Juvenile Justice System—Progress and Problems. Washington, DC: U.S. Department of Justice.

BESHAROV, D. J. (1974) Juvenile Justice Advocacy. New York: Practicing Law Institute.

BITTNER, E. (1970) The Functions of the Police in Modern Society. Washington, DC: Government Printing Office.

BLACK, D. (1980) The Manners and Customs of the Police. New York: Academic Press.

BLACK, D. and A. J. REISS, Jr. (1970) "Police control of juveniles." American Sociological Review 35 (February): 63-77.

BUCKNER, J. C. and M. CHESNEY-LIND (1983) "Dramatic cures for juvenile crime: an evaluation of a prisoner-run delinquency prevention program." Criminal Justice and Behavior 10, 2: 227-247.

Bureau of Justice Statistics (1982a) The 1982 Jail Census. Washington, DC: Government Printing Office.

————(1982b) Jail Inmates 1982. Washington, DC: U.S. Department of Justice.

————(1983) Report to the Nation on Crime and Justice. Washington, DC: U.S. Department of Justice.

————(1983) Sourcebook of Criminal Justice Statistics. Washington, DC: U.S. Government Printing Office.

CALDWELL, R. G. (1961) "The juvenile court: its development and some major problems." Journal of Criminal Law, Criminology and Police Science 51: 493-511.

CAVENDER, G. (1981) "Scared straight! ideology and the media." Journal of Criminal Justice 9, 6: 431-440.

CHAMBLISS, W. J. (1984) "The saints and the roughnecks," pp. 126-135 in W. J. Chambliss (ed.) Criminal Law in Action. New York: John Wiley.

CHESNEY-LIND, M. (1977) "Judicial paternalism and the female status offender." Crime and Delinquency 23 (April): 121-130.

————(1982) "Guilty by reason of sex: young women and the juvenile justice system," pp. 77-103 in B. R. Price and N. J. Sokoloff (eds.) The Criminal Justice System and Women. New York: Clark Boardman.

Children's Defense Fund (1976) Children in Adult Jails. New York: Washington Research Project.

COATES, R. B., A. D. MILLER, and L. E. OHLIN (1978) Diversity in a Youth Correctional System: Handling Delinquents in Massachusetts. Cambridge, MA: Ballinger.

COFFEY, A. R. (1974) Juvenile Justice as a System: Law Enforcement to Rehabilitation. Englewood Cliffs, NJ: Prentice-Hall.

COHEN, L. E. (1975a) Pre-Adjudicatory Detention in Three Juvenile Courts. Washington, DC: Government Printing Office.

————(1975b) Juvenile Dispositions: Social and Legal Factors Related to the Processing of Denver Delinquency Cases. Washington, DC: Government Printing Office.

Commission on Accreditation for Corrections (1978) Manual of Standards for Juvenile Probation and Aftercare Services. Rockville, MD: American Correctional Association.

CULBERTSON, R. G. (1975) "The effect of institutionalization on the delinquent inmate's self-concept." Journal of Criminal Law and Criminology 66, 1: 88-93.

CULLEN, F. T., K. M. GOLDEN, and J. B. CULLEN (1983) "Is child saving dead? attitudes toward rehabilitation in Illinois." Journal of Criminal Justice 11, 1: 1-14.

DAVIS, S. M. (1974) Rights of Juveniles: The Juvenile Justice System. New York: Clark Boardman.

DEL CARMEN, R. V. (1985) "Legal issues and liabilities in community corrections," pp. 47-70 in L. F. Travis III (ed.) Probation, Parole, and Community Corrections. Prospect Heights, IL: Waveland.

DE MAUSE, L. (1974) The History of Childhood. New York: Psychohistory Press.

ELDEFONSO, E. and W. HARTINGER (1976) Control, Treatment and Rehabilitation of Juvenile Offenders. Encino, CA: Glencoe.

EMPEY, L. T. (1982) American Delinquency: Its Meaning and Construction. Homewood, IL: Dorsey Press.

ERICKSON, M. (1973) "Group violations and official delinquency: the group hazard hypothesis." Criminology 11 (August): 127-160.

FARE v. MICHAEL C. (1979) 99 S. Ct. 2560.

FELD, B. C. (1978) "Reference of juvenile offenders for adult prosecution: the legislative alternative to asking unanswerable questions." Minnesota Law Review 62: 515-618.

———(1981) "Legislative policies toward the serious juvenile offender." Crime and Delinquency 27: 497-521.

———(1983) "Delinquent careers and criminal policy: just deserts and the waiver decision." Criminology 21: 195-212.

FENWICK, C. R. (1982) "Juvenile court intake decision-making: the importance of family affiliation." Journal of Criminal Justice 10: 443-453.

FEYERHERM, W. (1980) "The group hazard hypothesis: a re-examination." Journal of Research in Crime and Delinquency 17 (January): 58-68.

FINCKENAUER, J. O (1982) Scared Straight! and the Panacea Phenomenon. Englewood Cliffs, NJ: Prentice-Hall.

FOX, S. J. (1977) Juvenile Courts in a Nutshell. St. Paul, MN: West.

GASPER, J. and D. KATKIN (1980) "A rationale for the abolition of the juvenile court's power to waive jurisdiction." Pepperdine Law Review 7 (Summer): 939-951.

In re Gault (1967) 387 U.S. 1.

GIBBONS, D. and G. BLAKE (1978) "Evaluating the impact of juvenile diversion programs." Crime and Deliquency 22 (October): 411-420.

GILLIS, J. (1974) Youth and History. New York: Academic Press.

GLASER, D. (1973) Routinizing Evaluation: Getting Feedback on the Effectiveness of Crime and Delinquency Programs. Rockville, MD: National Institute of Mental Health.

GOLDSTEIN, H. (1977) Policing a Free Society. Cambridge, MA: Ballinger.

GRIMES, C. (1983) Girls and the Law. Washington, DC: Institute for Education Leadership.

HAMPARIAN, D. M., R. S. SCHUSTER, S. DINITZ, and J. P. CONRAD (1978) The Violent Few: A Study of Dangerous Juvenile Offenders. Lexington, MA: D. C. Heath.

HAMPARIAN, D. M., L. K. ESTEP, S. M. MUNTEAN, R. R. PRESTINO, R. G. SWISHER, P. L. WALLACE, and J. L. WHITE (1982) Youth in Adult Court: Between Two Worlds. Washington, DC: U.S. Department of Justice, Office of Juvenile Justice and Delinquency Prevention, National Institute for Juvenile Justice and Delinquency Prevention.

HINDELANG, M. J. (1976) "With a little help from their friends: group participation in reported delinquent behavior." British Journal of Criminology 16, 2: 109-125.

HINDELANG, M. J., T. HIRSCHI, and J. G. WEIS (1981) Measuring Delinquency. Beverly Hills, CA: Sage.

HIRSCHI, T., M. J. HINDELANG, and J. G. WEIS (1980) "The status of self-report measures," pp. 473-488 in M. W. Klein and K. S. Teilmann (eds.) Handbook of Criminal Justice Evaluation. Beverly Hills, CA: Sage.

HOFFMAN, P. B. and B. STONE-MEIERHOFFER (1980) "Reporting recidivism rates: the criterion and follow-up issues." Journal of Criminal Justice 8: 53-60.

HOHENSTEIN, W. F. (1969) "Factors influencing the police disposition of juvenile offenders," pp. 138-149 in T. Sellin and M. E. Wolfgang (eds.) Delinquency: Selected Studies. New York: John Wiley.

HOMANT, R. J. (1981) "The demise of JOLT: the politics of being scared straight in Michigan." Criminal Justice Review 6: 14-18.

HOWLETT, F. W. (1973) "Is the Youth Service Bureau all it's cracked up to be?" Crime and Delinquency 19 (October): 485-492.

HUNTINGTON, J. F. (1982) "Powerless and vulnerable: the social experiences of imprisoned girls." Juvenile and Family Court Journal 33, 2: 33-44.

HUSSEY, F. A. (1976) "Perspectives on parole decision-making with juveniles." Criminology 13, 4: 449-470.

JOHNSON, T. A. (1975) Introduction to the Juvenile Justice System. St. Paul, MN: West.

JONES, C. T. and M. KRAVITZ (1980) Variations on Juvenile Probation: A Selected Bibliography. Washington, DC: Government Printing Office.

KENNEY, J. P., D. G. PURSUIT, D. E. FULLER, and R. F. BARRY (1982) Police Work with Juveniles and the Administration of Juvenile Justice. Springfield, IL: Charles C Thomas.

KENT v. UNITED STATES (1966) 383 U.S. 541.

KESSEN, W. (1965) The Child. New York: John Wiley.

KLEIN, M. W. (1976) "Issues and realities in police diversion programs." Crime and Delinquency 22 (October): 421-427.

———(1981) "On frustration tolerance and self-flagellation: the decision to evaluate," pp. 249-261 in W. S. Davidson, J. R. Koch, R. G. Lewis, and M. D. Wresinski (eds.) Evaluation Strategies in Criminal Justice. Elmsford, NY: Pergamon Press.

———and K. S. TEILMANN (1980) "Pivotal ingredients of police juvenile diversion programs," pp. 168-180 in H. T. Rubin (ed.) Juveniles in Justice: A Book of Readings. Santa Monica, CA: Goodyear.

———J. A. STYLES, S. B. LINCOLN, and S. LABIN-ROSENWEIG (1976) "The explosion in police diversion programs: evaluating the structural dimensions of a social fad," pp. 101-119 in M. W. Klein (ed.) The Juvenile Justice System. Beverly Hills, CA: Sage.

KLOCKARS, C. (1985) The Idea of Police. Beverly Hills, CA: Sage.

KOBETZ, R. W. and B. B. BOSARGE (1973) Juvenile Justice Administration. Gaithersburg, MD: International Association of Chiefs of Police.

KOBRIN, S. and M. KLEIN (1982) National Evaluation of the Deinstitutionalization of Status Offender Programs—Executive Summary. Washington, DC: National Institute of Justice.

LAMB v. BROWN (1972) 456 F.2d 18.

LATESSA, E. J., L. F. TRAVIS III, and G. P. WILSON (1984) "Juvenile diversion: factors related to decision making and outcome," pp. 145-165 in S. H. Decker (ed.) Juvenile Justice Policy: Analyzing Trends and Outcomes. Beverly Hills, CA: Sage.

LERMAN, P. (1975) Community Treatment and Social Control: A Critical Analysis of Juvenile Correctional Policy. Chicago: University of Chicago Press.

LERMAN, P. (1979) "Order offenses and juvenile delinquency," pp. 150-180 in L. T. Empey (ed.) Juvenile Justice: The Progressive Legacy and Current Reforms. Charlottesville: University Press of Virginia.

LEWIS, R. V. (1983) "Scared straight—California style: evaluation of the San Quentin Squires Program." Criminal Justice and Behavior 10, 2: 209-226.

LUNDMAN, R. J. (1976) "Will diversion reduce recidivism?" Crime and Delinquency 22 (October): 428-437.

LUNDMAN, R. J. and F. R. SCARPITTI (1978) "Delinquency prevention: recommendations for future projects." Crime and Delinquency 22 (April): 207-220.

LUNDMAN, R. J., P. T. McFARLAND, and F. R. SCARPITTI (1976) "Delinquency prevention: a description and assessment of projects reported in the professional literature." Crime and Delinquency 20 (July): 297-308.

LUNDMAN, R. J., R. E. SYKES, and J. P. CLARK (1980) "Police control of juveniles: a replication," pp. 130-151 in R. J. Lundman (ed.) Police Behavior: A Sociological Perspective. New York: Oxford University Press.

MARSHALL, F. H. and G. F. VITO (1982) "Not without the tools: the task of probation in the eighties." Federal Probation 46, 3: 37-40.

MARTINSON, R. M. (1974) "What works? questions and answers about prison reform." The Public Interest 35 (Spring): 22-54.

————(1976) "California research at the crossroads." Crime and Delinquency 22 (April): 180-191.

MASSACHUSETTS v. SHEPARD (1984) 104 S.Ct. 3424.

MATHIAS, R. A. [ed.] (1984) Violent Juvenile Offenders: An Anthology. San Francisco: National Council on Crime and Delinquency.

MORASH, M. (1984) "Establishment of a juvenile record: the influence of individual and peer group characteristics." Criminology 22, 1: 97-112.

MURRAY, C. A. and L. A. COX (1979) Beyond Probation: Juvenile Corrections and the Chronic Delinquent. Beverly Hills, CA: Sage.

MLYNIEL, W. J. (1976) "Juvenile delinquent or adult convict: the prosecutor's choice." American Criminal Law Review 14: 29-57.

McKEIVER v. PENNSYLVANIA (1971) 403 U.S. 528.

McNEECE, C. A. (1980) "Deinstitutionalization of juvenile status offenders: new myths and old realities." Journal of Sociology and Social Welfare 7, 2: 236-245.

National Advisory Commission on Criminal Justice Standards Goals (1976) Juvenile Justice and Delinquency Prevention: Report of the Task Force on Juvenile Justice and Delinquency Prevention. Washington, DC: U.S. Department of Justice.

National Center for Juvenile Justice (1982) "1979 juvenile justice system model." p. 19 in Facts About Youth and Delinquency. Washington, DC: National Institute of Juvenile Justice and Delinquency Prevention.

National Center for Juvenile Justice (1982) "1979 juvenile justice system model," p. 19 serious offenders: 38 recommendations." Juvenile & Family Court Journal (Summer): 1-24.

National Council on Crime and Delinquency (1971) Secure Juvenile Detention Needs in Upper New York State. New York: Author.

NEJELSKI, P. (1976) "Diversion: the promise and the danger." Crime and Delinquency 22 (October): 393-410.

————and J. LA POOK (1974) "Monitoring the juvenile justice system: How can you tell where you're going if you don't where you are?" American Criminal Law Review 13 (Summer): 14.

NELSON v. HEYNE (1974) 491 F. 2d. 352 7th Cir.

NETTLER, G. (1978) Explaining Crime. New York: McGraw-Hill.

NEW YORK v. QUARLES (1984) 104 S.Ct. 2626.

NORMAN, S. (1972) The Youth Service Bureau: A Key to Delinquency Prevention. San Francisco: National Council on Crime and Delinquency.

Office of Juvenile Justice and Delinquency Prevention (1983) Children in Custody: Advance Report on the 1982 Census of Public Juvenile Facilities. Washington, DC: Government Printing Office.

OSBUN, L. A. and P. A. RODE (1984) "Prosecuting juveniles as adults: the quest for 'objective' decisions." Criminology 22: 187-202.

PACKER, H. L. (1968) The Limits of the Criminal Sanction. Stanford, CA: Stanford University Press.

PALMER, T. B. (1971) "California's community treatment program for delinquent adolescents." Journal of Research in Crime and Delinquency 8 (January): 74-92.

PALMER, T. B. (1975) "Martinson revisited." Journal of Research in Crime and Delinquency 12 (July): 133-152.

In re Patricia A. (1972) 31 N.Y.2d 83; 335 N.Y.S.2d 33.

PAUL, W. N. and H. S. WATT (1980) Deinstitutionalization of Status Offenders: A Compilation and Analysis of State Statutes. Denver: State Legislative Leaders Foundation.

PAULSEN, M. G. and C. H. WHITEBREAD (1974) Juvenile Law and Procedure. Reno, NV: National Council of Juvenile Court Judges.

PAWLAK, E. J. (1972) "The administration of juvenile justice" Ph.D. dissertation, University of Michigan, Ann Arbor.

———(1977) "Differential selection of juveniles for detention." Journal of Research on Crime and Delinquency 14 (July): 1-12.

Pennsylvania Joint Council on the Criminal Justice System (1978) The Transfer of Juveniles to Adult Courts in Pennsylvania. Harrisburg, PA: Author.

PEPINSKY, H. E. (1980) Crime Control Strategies: An Introduction to the Study of Crime. New York: Oxford University Press.

PILIAVIN, I. and S. BRIAR (1964) "Police encounters with juveniles." American Journal of Sociology 70 (September): 206-214.

POOLE, E. D. and R. M. REGOLI (1983) "Violence in juvenile institutions: a comparative study." Criminology 21, 2: 213-232.

President's Commission on Law Enforcement and the Administration of Justice (1967) Corrections. Washington, DC: Government Printing Office.

President's Commission on Law Enforcement and the Administration of Justice (1967) Task Force Report: Juvenile Delinquency and Youth Crime. Washington, DC: Government Printing Office.

REISS, A. J., Jr. (1971) The Police and the Public. New Haven, CT: Yale University Press.

REUTERMAN, N. A. and T. R. HUGHES (1984) "Developments in juvenile justice during the decade of the 70s: juvenile detention facilities." Journal of Criminal Justice 12, 4: 325-334.

ROE v. CONN (1976) 417 F. Supp. 769 (M.D. Ala.).

ROSSI, P. H. and S. R. WRIGHT (1977) "Evaluation research: an assessment of theory, practice and politics." Evaluation Quarterly 1: 5-22.

ROTHMAN, D. J. (1980) Conscience and Convenience. Boston: Little, Brown.

———(1971) The Discovery of the Asylum. Boston: Little, Brown.

RUBENSTEIN, J. (1973) City Police. New York: Farrar, Straus & Giroux.

RUBIN, H. T. (1979) Juvenile Justice: Policy, Practice and Law. Santa Monica, CA: Goodyear.

———(1977) "The juvenile court's search for identity and responsibility." Crime and Delinquency 23 (January): 1-3.

SARRI, R. C. (1974) Under Lock and Key: Juveniles in Jails and Detention. National Assessment of Juvenile Corrections. Ann Arbor: University of Michigan.

SCARPITTI, F. R. and R. M. STEPHENSON (1968) "A study of probation effectiveness." Journal of Criminal Law, Criminology, and Police Science 59, 3: 361-369.

SCHNEIDER, A. (1984) "Sentencing guidelines and recidivism rates of juvenile offenders." Justice Quarterly 1, 1: 107-124.

SCHUR, E. (1973) Radical Non-Intervention: Rethinking the Delinquency Problem. Englewod Cliffs, NJ: Prentice-Hall.

SENNA, J. J. and L. J. SIEGEL (1981) Juvenile Delinquency: Theory, Practice, and Law. St. Paul, MN: West.

———(1976) Juvenile Law: Cases and Comments. St. Paul, MN: West.

SHEPARD, J. R. and D. M. ROTHENBERGER (1980) Police-Juvenile Diversion: An Alternative to Prosecution. Washington, DC: U.S. Department of Justice.

SIMONSEN, C. E. and M. S. GORDON III (1982) Juvenile Justice in America. New York: Macmillan.

SKOLNICK, J. (1964) Justice Without Trial. New York: John Wiley.

SPERGEL, I. A., F. G. REAMER, and J. P. LYNCH (1981) "Deinstitutionalization of status offenders—individual outcome and system effects." Journal of Research in Crime and Delinquency 18: 4-33.

SPIRO, B. E. (1984) "Abolishing court jurisdiction over status offenders: anticipating the unintended consequences," pp. 77-94 in S. H. Decker (ed.) Juvenile Justice Policy: Analyzing Trends and Outcomes. Beverly Hills, CA: Sage.

STREIB, V. (1978) Juvenile Justice in America. Port Washington, NY: Kennikat Press.

SUCHMAN, E. (1967) Evaluation Research. New York: Russell Sage Foundation.

SUMNER, H. (1971) Locking Them Up: A Study of Juvenile Detention Decisions in Selected California Counties. San Francisco: National Council on Crime and Delinquency.

SUNDEEN, R. A., Jr. (1976) "Police professionalization and community attachments and diversion of juveniles," pp. 314-320 in R. M. Carter and M. W. Klein (eds.) Back on the Street: The Diversion of Juvenile Offenders. Englewood Cliffs, NJ: Prentice-Hall.

TERRY, R. M. (1967) "Discrimination in the handling of juvenile offenders by social control agencies." Journal of Research in Crime and Delinquency 4 (July): 218-230.

THORNBERRY, T. (1973) "Race, socioeconomic status, and sentencing in the juvenile justice system." Journal of Law and Criminology 64: 90-98.

TRACY, P. E. and R. M. FIGLIO (1982) "Chronic recidivism in the 1958 birth cohort." Paper presented at the annual meeting of the American Society of Criminology, Toronto, Canada.

Uniform Crime Reports for the United States (1983) Crime in the United States. Washington, DC: Government Printing Office.

UNITED STATES v. LEON (1984) 104 S.Ct. 3405.

VANAGUNAS, S. (1979) "Police diversion of juveniles: an ambiguous state of the art." Federal Probation 43, 3: 48-52.

VELIMESIS, M. (1969) Report on Survey of 41 Pennsylvania County Courts and Correctional Services for Women and Girl Offenders. Philadelphia: Pennsylvania Division of the American Association of University Women.

VITO, G. F. (1982) "Does it work? problems in the evaluation of a correctional treatment program." Journal of Offender Counseling, Services and Rehabilitation 7, 1: 5-22.

WADLINGTON, W., C. H. WHITEBREAD, and S. M. DAVIS (1983) Cases and Materials on Children in the Legal System. Mineola, NY: Foundation Press.

WALD, P. M. (1976) "Pretrial detention for juveniles," pp. 119-137 in M. K. Rosengeim (ed.) Pursuing Justice for the Child. Chicago: University of Chicago Press.

WEINER, N. L. and C. V. WILLIE (1971) "Decisions by juvenile officers." American Journal of Sociology 77, 2: 199-210.

WEISS, C. H. (1975) "Evaluation research in the political context," pp. 13-26 in E. L. Struening and M. Guttentag (eds.) Handbook of Evaluation Research. Beverly Hills, CA: Sage.

WEST v. UNITED STATES (1968) 399 F.2d 467.

In re Whittington (1968) 391 U.S. 341.

WILKINS, L. T. (1969) Evaluation of Penal Measures. New York: Random House.

WILSON, J. Q. (1968a) "The police and the delinquent in two cities," pp. 9-30 in S. Wheeler (ed.) Controlling Delinquents. New York: John Wiley.

———(1968b) Varieties of Police Behavior. Cambridge, MA: Harvard University Press.

In re Winship (1970) 397 U.S. 358.

WOLFGANG, M. (1975) "Contemporary perspectives on violence," in D. Chappel and J. Monahan (eds.) Criminal Justice. Lexington, MA: D. C. Heath.

———(1977) "From boy to man—from delinquency to crime," in The Serious Juvenile Offender. Office of Juvenile Justice and Delinquency Prevention.

———R.M. FIGLIO and T. SELLIN (1972) Delinquency in a Birth Cohort. Chicago: University of Chicago Press.

WRIGHT, W. E. and M. C. DIXON (1978) "Community prevention and treatment of delinquency." Journal of Research in Crime and Delinquency 14 (January): 35-67.

YOUNG, T. M. and D. M. PAPPENFORT (1977) Secure Detention of Juveniles and Alternatives to Its Use. Washington, DC: National Institute of Justice.

INDEX

ABOUT THE AUTHORS

GENNARO F. VITO is Associate Professor in the School of Justice Administration (College of Urban and Public Affairs) at the University of Louisville. He received his Ph.D. in public administration from the Ohio State University in 1978. His publications on probation and parole and criminal justice evaluation research have appeared in several journals. He is the coauthor of *Probation and Parole in America.*

DEBORAH G. WILSON is Assistant Professor in the School of Justice Administration (College of Urban and Public Affairs) at the University of Louisville. She received her Ph.D. in sociology from Purdue University in 1980. Her other areas of interest include evaluation research and corrections. She is currently involved in research and program development for elderly and disabled inmates at the Kentucky State Reformatory.

NOTES